Bicycling the Blue Ridge

For Rosamond Foltyn and Anne Cornwall Johnson.

In memory of Willis David Johnson.

BICYCLING THE BLUE RIDGE

A GUIDE TO THE SKYLINE DRIVE
AND THE BLUE RIDGE PARKWAY

4TH EDITION

BY ELIZABETH AND CHARLIE SKINNER

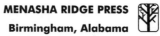

MENASHA RIDGE PRESS
Birmingham, Alabama

Library of Congress Cataloging-in-Publication Data

Skinner, Elizabeth, 1962–
Bicycling the Blue Ridge: A Guide to the Skyline Drive and the
Blue Ridge Parkway/ by Elizabeth and Charlie Skinner.—4th ed.
   p. cm.
Includes bibliographical references and index.
ISBN 0-89732-561-3
1. Bicycle touring—Virginia—Skyline Drive—Guidebooks.
2. Bicycle touring—Blue Ridge Parkway (N.C. and Va.)—
Guidebooks. 3. Skyline Drive (Va.)—Guidebooks. 4. Blue Ridge
Parkway (N.C. and Va.)—Guidebooks. I. Skinner, Charlie, 1943–
II. Title

GV1045.5.V82S626   2004
796.6'4'097559—dc22
                                                      2004042655

Menasha Ridge Press
P.O. Box 43673
Birmingham, AL 35243
www.menasharidge.com

Photography by Elizabeth and Charlie Skinner, Dennis Coello, and
Bud Zehmer
Cover photography by Dennis Coello
Cover and text design by Grant M. Tatum
Cartography by Grant M. Tatum, Steve Jones, and Bud Zehmer

Contents

Part 3: Appendices

Acknowledgments

We would like to thank the exceptional people who helped make this book possible. Former Menasha staff members Kate Dunlap, Anne Kennedy, Jessica Letteney, and Laura Mansberg were all instrumental in shaping the first edition. Our good friends Kathleen and Fred Wheeless served as sounding boards for our ideas and provided needed assistance with photography. The original data for the elevation profiles was developed by Jeff Patton, associate professor of Geography at the University of North Carolina at Greensboro, and further enhanced by Bud Zehmer, who, on behalf of Menasha Ridge Press, also performed extensive research and editing for this fourth edition. Thanks to Grant M. Tatum, whose talent in graphic design brings a crisp look to the interior of the book. New photographs by Dennis Coello and Bud Zehmer spruce up the new edition. Thanks to editor Gabbie Oates for her efforts in the creation of the fourth edition. As always, we are indebted to our family for their love and support.

—Elizabeth Skinner

Preface

There is no ribbon of highway more ideal for bicycling than the Skyline Drive and the Blue Ridge Parkway. Perhaps we feel this way because we stubbornly seek out roads that are enticing to the senses and physically challenging. We spent the greater part of our lives in Florida, a state summed up by bicyclists as hot, flat, and full of headwinds. There is no fall season in Florida; it's pretty much green there year-round. So, bicycling against a backdrop of yellow, russet, and orange was a new experience for us. After five years of exploration by bicycle, the Blue Ridge continues to amaze us.

Now let us concede from the beginning, the Skyline Drive and the Blue Ridge Parkway are never easy. You simply cannot be a passive cyclist on these roads. You work excruciatingly hard climbing its mountains, but the descents are more thrilling than your favorite roller-coaster ride. They're scarier too, for the controls are all yours. All senses are alert. Body and machine meet rubber and pavement in a high-voltage connection.

Cycling on the Skyline Drive and the Blue Ridge Parkway can be a humbling experience. The bicyclist who attempts these roads

Elizabeth and Charlie pause at a scenic overlook of the Shenandoah Valley.

has definitely signed up for some tough mountain cycling. If the worst hill you've tackled is that bridge or overpass in your otherwise flat hometown, you are in for a big shock. We will address this matter of hill climbing later. First, a word about what motivated us to write this book.

In our travels on the Skyline Drive and the Blue Ridge Parkway we have met cyclists from France, Japan, California, Florida, and Texas, all in varying stages of bewilderment and frustration. The Skyline Drive and the Blue Ridge Parkway present special challenges to the cyclist. In addition to steep road grades, weather conditions are often a menace. Rain, fog, and gusty winds are possible. Facilities are set up for the convenience of the car traveler. Food stops may simply be too far apart to be practical for the bicyclist. Since the Park Service allows no advertising on the Skyline Drive and the Blue Ridge Parkway, motels, restaurants, medical facilities, and the like are often hidden.

Facilities as close as a half mile off the Parkway may be completely concealed from view. Even the literature that outlines facilities off the Skyline Drive and the Blue Ridge Parkway is almost exclusively designed for the car traveler. We have learned the hard way about turning off the Parkway only to find ourselves in an immediate descent to nowhere. This means only one thing: a tough climb back up the side of a mountain. And we *like* to climb. If only there were a traveler's guide written for bicyclists from their point of view.

We wrote this book with three groups of bicyclists in mind: racers, long-distance touring cyclists, and recreational cyclists. The Blue Ridge Parkway and the Skyline Drive have much to offer each group. Of course, many bicyclists cross over between categories.

Overall, this book is designed for the touring bicyclist who plans to ride the Skyline Drive and the Blue Ridge Parkway in an extended tour. In our view, this approach maximizes the experience. However, nothing is more gratifying than a hard ride with just you, your racing bike, and the mountains—no gear, no hassles. We live in Winston-Salem, North Carolina, and a single Sunday ride on the Blue Ridge Parkway can sustain us at least until the next weekend.

If you are a racer, you may not care about campgrounds and motels, but you probably appreciate knowing where the country stores and other food stops are. We can think of no better training ground for a racer than these roads.

Part of the fun of bicycle touring is making discoveries along the way. We do not want to take any mystery away from this. Our hope is that this book can enhance your experience. As the touring cyclist, you still have the excitement of coming upon the delights of the area, but perhaps you won't find yourself famished because of a ten-mile miscalculation over the next food stop. Glendale Springs Restaurant and Inn is only a half-mile from the Parkway, but you would never know of its gastronomic promise as you cruised past Milepost 260.

DISCLAIMER

Bicyclists assume responsibility for their own safety each time they undertake a bicycle trip. No guidebook can alert you to up-to-the-minute changes in weather, traffic, and road conditions. Each cyclist should consider his or her own abilities when planning a bicycle tour of the Blue Ridge. We strongly urge you to wear a helmet.

May all your cycling adventures be safe and bursting with fun, thrills, and excitement.

PART 1:
AN INTRODUCTION
TO BICYCLING
THE BLUE RIDGE

The Ultimate Bicycling Road

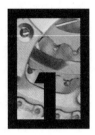

For the bicyclist, the Blue Ridge Parkway and the Skyline Drive
present an impressive list of statistics. Combined, these two highways comprise 575 miles of continuous road, which rides the crest
of the Blue Ridge Mountains. The Blue Ridge Mountains are the
eastern rampart of the Appalachian Mountains extending from
southern Pennsylvania to northern Georgia. The Skyline Drive and
the Blue Ridge Parkway enable the bicyclist to experience a large
portion of the Blue Ridge Mountains. These two roads can transport
you from Front Royal, Virginia (just 67 miles from Washington,
D.C.), to Cherokee in the southwest corner of North Carolina at the
gateway of the Great Smoky Mountains National Park. The Skyline
Drive extends 105 miles from Front Royal to Rockfish Gap just out-
side Waynesboro, Virginia. At Rockfish Gap the road continues
uninterrupted as the Blue Ridge Parkway.

Although elevations in the Blue Ridge are modest compared
to the Rockies or the Sierra Nevada, changes in elevation on
the Skyline Drive and the Parkway are fairly irregular. The highest

elevation on the Skyline Drive and the Blue Ridge Parkway (hereafter referred to as "the Parkway") is 6,053 feet at Richland Balsam in the Great Balsams between Mount Pisgah and Cherokee. The next highest elevations are in the Black Mountain range, which is in the southernmost section of the Parkway. One of the most exhilarating side trips off either road is the five-mile climb to the summit of Mount Mitchell, which at 6,684 feet is the highest point in the eastern United States. The lowest point of the roads is near Otter Creek in Virginia, at 649 feet.

After many talks with bicyclists on the Parkway and the Skyline Drive, we think it is fair to say that changes in elevation are a major preoccupation with bicyclists who undertake the Blue Ridge. If we have learned nothing else in our thousands of miles logged on the Parkway and the Skyline Drive, it is that cycling is much more enjoyable if you can somehow manage to suspend all worry about elevation and just take it as it comes. Conceding that elevation is critical to cyclists, we have detailed changes in elevation in our point-by-point descriptive section.

Mabry Mill is popular for good reason—a tour of the mill is fascinating!

The Blue Ridge Mountains have a rich geologic history. As a part of the Appalachian mountain range, the Blue Ridge Mountains are among the oldest mountains on earth. As you cycle past sheer granite walls, some blasted through in the construction of these roads, think about the amount of time Precambrian rock represents: the geologic upheaval that formed the Appalachian mountain range took place about 200 million years ago during the Paleozoic era.

For bicyclists, wind is often the dominant element dictating the pace and the effort required to travel from point A to point B. The wind has smoothed and carved the Blue Ridge over millions of years. Angles here are not severe and jagged like the Rockies, but windswept and misty with mosses, wildflowers, balsam, rhododendron, and mountain laurel that seem to ease the mountain back to earth. Edward Abbey brings the geologic history of the Appalachians to its logical conclusion in *Appalachian Wilderness*:

> What the future holds for the mountains, according to geology, is simply a long continuation of the present erosional downgrading which will end, presumably, given enough time and if the world lasts that long, with the Appalachians as we know them reduced to a more or less featureless peneplain—to no more, that is, than a gently rolling surface of rock and field and forest (we hope) not much above sea level.

We are lucky to have these mountains here in the South. People gravitate to the timelessness and calm of the Blue Ridge for renewal and refuge. Interestingly, Great Smoky Mountains National Park happens to be the most heavily visited park in the National Park System.

Before any talk of national parks, history chronicles the people who settled in the Blue Ridge. Many of these people were of Scotch-Irish descent, and other settlers were German immigrants from the Black Forest, who introduced techniques for building cabins like those of their homeland. All who persisted and survived the rugged conditions and isolation of the Blue Ridge surmounted many obstacles. The folklore and specialized knowledge these mountain people possessed are now celebrated as a unique and important heritage.

Opportunities for reflection on the culture of the Blue Ridge are readily available along the Skyline Drive and the Parkway. The National Park Service has designed displays, signs, and visitor centers to illustrate the lifestyle of the early settlers. There are several sites that demonstrate the daily life of the mountain culture. The working farm at Humpback Rocks Visitor Center is run by Park Service staff who dress in period costume and tend the farm using early methods. The gristmill at Mabry Mill operates year-round: There is no better place to see authentic apparatus used to make sorghum, molasses, and apple butter during the fall season. Caudill Cabin, visible in the Doughton Park area, invites the traveler to speculate on the isolation of existence in the Blue Ridge.

Anyone who spends even a week bicycle-touring the Blue Ridge can experience a hint of the vulnerability early settlers experienced in this unyielding, sparsely populated area. Although the mountains are becoming increasingly developed in tourist areas, the Parkway and the Skyline Drive continue to remain uncluttered by modern conveniences such as fast-food restaurants and mini-malls. For those, the Blue Ridge still requires us to descend from its peaks, however narrow National Park boundaries may be.

On the other hand, the Moses H. Cone Memorial Park and Mount Pisgah provide a glimpse into the wealth of the famous industrialists, Moses H. Cone and George Vanderbilt, both of whom built lavish mountain retreats. The contrast has always been great between subsistence farmers whose livelihood depends upon the mountains, and tourists who come to the Blue Ridge for sport and leisure.

The history of the construction of the Skyline Drive and the Parkway is rife with controversy. A number of proposed routes were mapped out before settling on the present one. The state of Tennessee campaigned heavily to host the Parkway, but ultimately lost out to North Carolina. The visionary behind a road that would connect Shenandoah National Park to Great Smoky Mountains

National Park is said to have been Virginia senator Harry F. Byrd. However, Theodore E. Straus, who was a public works administrator from Maryland, is also credited as the originator of the idea.

Officially, Franklin D. Roosevelt, Congress, the Virginia State Legislature, the people of Virginia and North Carolina, and the National Park Service were responsible for following through with the project. The Skyline Drive was begun through an Act of Congress. Due to the stipulation that no federal money be spent to acquire land for the Skyline Drive, the Virginia State Legislature appropriated over a million dollars and then solicited the people of Virginia to donate land and matching funds. The Civilian Conservation Corps completed the Skyline Drive in 1939.

President Roosevelt was so pleased by the success of the Skyline Drive that he approved a joint project by the National Park Service and the Bureau of Public Roads to connect Shenandoah

On an excursion into Asheville, this cyclist discovers City/County Park, site of many annual festivals, and an obelisk dedicated to a Civil War governor.

National Park with Great Smoky Mountains National Park. The Blue Ridge Parkway was not officially completed until 1987 with the opening of the Linn Cove Viaduct. Before its completion travelers had to take a brief detour in the Boone–Blowing Rock area to circumvent privately owned Grandfather Mountain.

Although the Linn Cove Viaduct is celebrated as an engineering marvel, the entire Skyline Drive and Parkway project is masterful. It is astounding that so many diverse groups of people came together to build the mountain highway: politicians who were immersed in their agendas, government officials who oversaw the project, highway engineers and landscape architects who were focused on the path of the road, mountain folk who were employed by the Civilian Conservation Corps during the Depression, skilled artisans from Europe who crafted the elegant stone bridges and tunnels, landowners who were coaxed into selling their land, and naturalists who were concerned with the environmental impact of the road.

Since this book champions what the Parkway and the Skyline Drive have to offer bicyclists, there are four simple facts that make these roads ideal for our mode of travel. There are no route changes to contend with; the road surface is well above average; commercial traffic is prohibited; and the speed limit is much lower than a regular highway.

There are no route changes. The Skyline Drive makes a seamless transition into the Blue Ridge Parkway at Rockfish Gap, Virginia. If you are traveling north, you will be required to pay a small fee upon entering the Skyline Drive from the Parkway. The Skyline Drive is a toll road and fees are collected at all entrance stations. This entitles you to seven days of travel along the Skyline Drive.

From time to time, we have been disoriented on whether to head north or south when driving or cycling up onto the Parkway from an entrance ramp. When you enter at random from a highway that intersects the Parkway, you encounter a sign that states simply: Blue Ridge Parkway (with arrows pointing north or south). You must proceed in one direction in order to find a sign that

One of the many beautiful overlooks in North Carolina.

states a destination and its mileage. The Skyline Drive has four designated entry points: Front Royal, Virginia, the northernmost entry point; followed by Thornton Gap; Swift Run Gap; and Rockfish Gap. Signage is very clear at all of these points.

The road surface on both highways is excellent. However, conditions do change with time. For example, during one season the Park Service upgraded much of the drainage system and some of the overlooks along the Skyline Drive. This meant several construction sites caused traffic to be routed onto a single lane. The Twin Tunnels were being repaired on the Parkway. The Park Service was also doing major roadwork between Asheville and Mount Pisgah. These are all situations where the Park Service was in the process of maintaining and upgrading the road.

If you are concerned about problems with road conditions, we suggest you call ahead of time for a current report on ongoing construction. For conditions along the Skyline Drive, call for information at (540) 999-3500; and along the Parkway, call (828) 298-0398. You can visit the Blue Ridge website, www.blueridgeskyline.com. You can also ask a park ranger upon arrival at either Park. For emergencies, call (800) 732-0911.

Stone mileposts are positioned at each mile on both the Skyline Drive and the Blue Ridge Parkway.

Although the Park Service actively maintains these roads, weather and erosion can create temporary problems. Fallen rocks, broken limbs or fallen trees, dead animals, and roads slick with rain or ice are potential hazards. The Park Service has posted signs in falling rock zones. You will also find warning signs for deer crossings and signs announcing all tunnels.

Both roads are clearly marked with signs denoting overlooks, campgrounds, picnic areas, ranger stations, intersecting highways, elevation points, hiking trails, and any other facilities sponsored by the National Park Service. The Park Service prohibits all advertising along these roads. Some enterprising business people perch signs on hillsides beyond park boundaries, hopeful that travelers will spot them as they gaze at the countryside. In many cases, country stores and motels go unnoticed even though they are less than a mile from the road.

One sign that carries great significance for bicyclists is the milepost marker. Stone mileposts are positioned at each mile on both the Skyline Drive and the Parkway. Just as you can get hung up on elevation, anticipating every mile is no fun either. They are hard to miss, though. Most of us probably register every single marker subconsciously, and they are indispensable in charting your way through the Blue Ridge. It's not likely you will ever get lost on the Skyline Drive or the Parkway.

There is no paved shoulder or bicycle lane on either road, but we have never felt this to be a great loss. The road is amply wide enough for a car and a bike. The only vehicles that sometimes cause problems are RVs and their drivers who sometimes underestimate the size of their vehicles on the road.

Also, beware of wide mirrors on pickups or vehicles towing campers. The full length of some people's camping entourage is amazing and from a bicyclist's perspective, insane. It is common to see a full-sized pickup truck pulling not only an Airstream camper but also a car for sightseeing—the total camping unit. As horrific as this sounds, we can deal with it when we consider that the maximum speed limit on the Skyline Drive is 35 mph and only 45 mph on the Parkway. Do keep in mind that "scenic highway" implies tourist traffic. The majority of travelers on these roads are there to sightsee. Drivers are not always paying attention to their driving. Cars occasionally come to abrupt stops or suddenly pull off the road: erratic behavior is common.

Never having to worry about commercial truck traffic is a major advantage that the Skyline Drive and the Parkway offer bicyclists. We all cope with adverse conditions on unrestricted roads, so not having to worry about ten tons of steel looming from behind is very liberating. Even if you are highly selective about the roads you cycle, a highway that prohibits commercial traffic is rare. You may encounter occasional delivery trucks headed for one of the Park Service concessions, but they take the most expedient route on and off these roads.

There are two primary differences between the Skyline Drive and the Blue Ridge Parkway. The Skyline Drive is a toll road, and elevations on the Skyline Drive do not reach the extremes of those on the Parkway. The highest point on the Skyline Drive is 3,680 feet. Generally, the Skyline Drive rides a plateau. Once you have climbed up to the 3,000-foot range, you will find markedly less variation in elevation than on the Parkway until you descend at either end. By comparison, the Parkway has wild variations in elevation. In a 30-mile stretch from Otter Creek to the Peaks of Otter, you cycle from the lowest point on the Parkway in Virginia at 649 feet to the highest point on the Parkway in Virginia at 3,950 feet.

One other difference between the Skyline Drive and the Parkway is the number of Park Service concessions. The Skyline Drive has an abundance of restaurants, campgrounds, and lodges well spaced for bicyclists. The Parkway is less consistent: Park Service concessions are as close together as 35 miles and as far apart as 70 miles. Careful planning is not only smart, but also necessary.

The Park Service has put some thought into the reality of bicyclists and motorists coexisting on the Parkway and the Skyline Drive by announcing in their literature and signage the necessity that motorists be alert to bicyclists. For example, bicycle-warning signs are present at the opening of each of the 27 tunnels on the Parkway and the single tunnel on the Skyline Drive.

Visibility in these tunnels is cause for concern and should be taken seriously. None of the tunnels have artificial lighting, so the longer tunnels are pitch black inside. Even when using lights we have felt out of control in some tunnels, especially those south of Waterrock Knob near Cherokee. The descent in this area ranges from 5,718 feet to 2,020 feet. Just imagine entering these tunnels from bright sunshine at speeds between 30 and 45 mph. Suddenly, you've lost the edge of the road and everything is black. You're still seeing the afterglow of the sun. Oh no, you hear something large and heavy rumbling up ahead. It's probably an RV. You're getting very unsure of yourself very fast. In the section on equipment, we discuss how to prepare for tunnels.

We feel that bicyclists could command greater respect for their rights if they did their part to share the road with cars. In fact, the Park Service has published guidelines and warnings about road conditions for bicyclists:

BICYCLING REGULATIONS:

◆ Bicycle riders must comply with all applicable state and federal motor vehicle regulations.

◆ Bicycles may be ridden only on paved road surfaces and parking areas. Bicycles, including mountain bikes, may not be ridden on trails or walkways.

◆ The bicycle operator must exhibit a white light or reflector visible at least 500 feet to the front and a red light or reflector visible at least 200 feet to the rear during periods of low visibility between the hours of sunset and sunrise, or while traveling through a tunnel.

◆ Bicycles must be ridden single file (except when passing or turning left) and well to the right-hand side of the road.

◆ Bicycle speed must be reasonable for control with regard to traffic, weather, road, and light conditions.

FOR SAFE BICYCLING:

◆ Wear a bicycle helmet.

◆ Be sure your bicycle is in good operating condition. Carry a spare tube and tools for minor repairs.

◆ Wear high-visibility clothing. It sets you apart from the scenery and makes you more noticeable to motorists.

◆ Avoid the Parkway during periods of low visibility. Fog and rain may occur unpredictably. Reschedule your trip for better weather or follow lower elevation routes until weather conditions improve.

◆ Exercise caution when riding through tunnels. Be sure your bicycle is equipped with proper lights or reflectors. There are 26 tunnels in North Carolina and 1 tunnel in Virginia.

◆ Temperatures vary greatly along the Parkway due to different elevations. Wear your clothing in layers.

- Safe drinking water is available at all picnic areas, campgrounds, concession operations, and visitor centers. Water from streams and springs is unsafe for drinking unless you purify it.
- Make an honest evaluation of your abilities before beginning a bicycle trip on the Parkway. In some sections, you will climb as much as 1,100 feet in 3.4 miles.
- When cycling in a group, adjust your spacing to allow motor vehicles to pass safely.

EXTENDED TRIPS:

- Some Parkway campgrounds and services are located too far apart for convenient cycling.
- Camping is permitted only at established campgrounds. In some areas, the U.S. Forest Service, state parks, and private campgrounds are within easy distance of the Parkway. However, many operate on a seasonal basis.
- Food and lodging services are also available along and adjacent to the Parkway. Most operate seasonally.
- To assist in planning your trip, consult the Parkway Map and Blue Ridge Parkway Directory.
- Carry a simple first-aid kit.
- Contact a ranger before leaving a motor vehicle parked overnight on the Parkway.

We think these guidelines are reasonable. Just remember how privileged we are to have such a road along the Blue Ridge. If you live for the ultimate road, this is it.

Weather in the Blue Ridge Mountains

Weather in the Blue Ridge Mountains has amazing, beautiful contrasts. Each season highlights special characteristics of the mountains. Bicycling in the southern Appalachians is great during much of the year, as long as you know what to expect, and prepare with the proper clothing. Weather can make or break a cycling trip in the Blue Ridge. That is true in any bicycling situation, but even more so in the mountains where weather fronts can move in suddenly, making weather a major consideration. Call (828) 298-0398 for up-to-date closures and weather-related info.

The Blue Ridge is famous for its display of fall colors. During autumn expect near bumper-to-bumper traffic, especially on the northern half of the Skyline Drive, which draws hordes of leaf peepers from the nearby Washington area. This is the biggest tourist time of the year. If you dislike competing with cars for your share of the road, we suggest you avoid weekends during peak leaf time.

Then November suddenly arrives with its wind and rain, which render the trees bare, and few care about the Blue Ridge except its true-blue aficionados. Houses usually hidden deep in the woods are revealed. Ridges and other physical features of the mountains rise up in relief. Fall days on the Parkway can be crisp and bright or overcast with a somber, damp chill that has you preferring a cozy fire to a brisk ride.

Winter is perhaps the most difficult season for the bicyclist, but it can be thrilling. From December through February (and sometimes into March), the Parkway may be best suited for cross-country skiing. Winter is certainly the most brutal season. The gnarled, stunted trees are a testament to winter's harsh winds. Snow and ice are treacherous. The Park Service closes off some sections of the road with gates barring car traffic.

Ice is the most serious hazard. We recommend mountain bikes in the winter months. There are steel-studded mountain bike tires for riding in snow and ice. Extended touring in the winter is not advised; day trips are more practical. Not only is the road difficult, but open facilities are scarce between November 1 and May 1. Just make sure you plan carefully and know the weather forecast before you venture out. Selected Park Service campgrounds are winterized and are open all winter.

Spring never seems to come soon enough for cyclists who have had to cope with bitter winter temperatures. This is aggravated by the spring's reputation for unpredictability. Even though it is officially spring on the calendar, the Blue Ridge may be destined for more weeks of bitter temperatures. During a recent March, we experienced a glorious weekend of cobalt blue skies when T-shirts and cycling shorts were the only clothing we required. The next weekend the temperature dropped thirty degrees, but we thought we could handle it. We had balaclavas, tights, polypropylene, and wind jackets, and we were truly miserable. The wind was devastating. If you drive up from the Piedmont or other lower elevations, remember that the mountains can easily be ten degrees cooler.

There is usually less rain in the spring. Although we cyclists can do without rain, lack of rain in the spring months can cause serious drought conditions in the Blue Ridge. Planning a cycling trip on the Blue Ridge is risky in early spring. You really need to keep a close eye on the weather forecast and know your tolerance level. Good weather or bad, the greatest challenge for cyclists in the spring is getting back in top form and toughing out the longer ascents.

Summer is the premier cycling season. Temperatures are warm, the foliage is lush and green, and wildflowers and rhododendron provide bright contrasts in color. When summer finally comes, it is a great feeling to shed all of those winter layers and cycle unencumbered by weight and bulk.

Summer in the Blue Ridge can be hot and humid; it can also be wet with sudden thunderstorms and fog. According to National Climatic Data Center statistics, the summer months are the foggiest of the year. In June, July, and August, there are an average of 11 days each month with less than a quarter-mile visibility due to heavy fog. August ranks highest with an average of 14 days of heavy fog; September comes in second with 12 days. Fog really can force you off of the Parkway and the Skyline Drive. We always tour with a flashing belt beacon for the rear of our bikes and a white light for the front. Visibility can be practically nil. The odds

Fall days on the Parkway can be crisp and bright or overcast with a somber, damp chill.

17

are high of encountering at least one morning or afternoon of inclement weather in a week's trip.

To illustrate the frustrations weather can cause cyclists, we would like to talk about September. We chose September twice in the past four years for extended cycling trips. One reason was that September, statistically, does not rank among the rainiest months in the Blue Ridge. The mean number of days with one-tenth of an inch or more of precipitation is eight. Eight to thirty, those odds don't sound too bad.

The first time we toured the entire length of the Skyline Drive and the Parkway, we experienced rain and fog every day for two weeks, from Front Royal, Virginia, to Blowing Rock, North Carolina. On our second September tour, the last 36 hours were a total rainout. The moral of the story: Weather in the Blue Ridge is unpredictable, so prepare for its downside. If you cannot handle cycling through rain, you will definitely need to factor in a few extra days into your travel itinerary.

One final aspect of the weather that you should be aware of is wind. Head winds are never much of a problem in the moun-

Wind gusting through gaps may surprise people who've never cycled in the mountains.

tains. The surprise for those who have never cycled in the mountains is wind gusting through gaps. Most gaps are labeled by signs along the Skyline Drive and the Parkway. In his *Blue Ridge Parkway Guide*, William G. Lord calls upon mountain folklore to define a gap:

> See the outline of that mountain over thar? Them low dips in it's what's knowed as a gap. Some of 'm is whar a road or trail is located acrost the mountains.

In general, the Parkway travels the crest line of the Blue Ridge and several other ranges. Therefore, it passes through a long series of gaps and intersects many cross-mountain roads.

On a windy day, gusts of wind may blow through these gaps in a mountain. You can be shooting down the side of a mountain only to find yourself fighting for control of your bike. A firm grip on the handlebars and confident bike-handling skills should prevent any mishaps.

On the final pages of this chapter, we have compiled data on temperature and precipitation available from the National Climatic Data Center in Asheville, North Carolina.

AVERAGE DAILY MAXIMUM AND MINIMUM TEMPERATURES (°F)

	Jan.	Feb.	Mar.	Apr.	May	June	July	Aug.	Sept.	Oct.	Nov.	Dec.
Asheville	47	51	58	69	76	81	84	83	78	69	59	50
	26	28	34	43	51	58	62	62	56	43	34	28
Boone	44	46	52	62	71	77	79	79	73	65	53	44
	25	25	31	38	47	55	59	58	51	41	32	25
Roanoke	45	48	57	68	76	83	87	85	79	69	57	48
	26	28	35	44	53	60	65	64	57	45	36	29
Peaks of Otter	n/a	n/a	n/a	64	72	77	81	79	73	63	n/a	n/a
	n/a	n/a	43	52	58	63	62	56	46	n/a	n/a	n/a
Big Meadows	n/a	n/a	n/a	59	67	74	76	75	69	60	n/a	n/a
	n/a	n/a	37	46	54	57	56	50	41	n/a	n/a	n/a

AVERAGE MONTHLY PRECIPITATION IN INCHES

	Jan.	Feb.	Mar.	Apr.	May	June	July	Aug.	Sept.	Oct.	Nov.	Dec.
Asheville	3.48	3.60	5.13	3.84	4.19	4.20	4.43	4.79	3.96	3.29	3.29	3.51
Boone	4.05	4.08	5.14	4.45	4.34	4.52	5.94	5.33	4.40	3.16	4.34	3.94
Roanoke	2.83	3.19	3.69	3.09	3.51	3.34	3.45	3.91	3.14	3.48	2.59	2.93
Peaks of Otter	n/a	n/a	n/a	n/a	n/a	n/a	n/a	5.50	n/a	3.51	n/a	n/a
Big Meadows	n/a	n/a	n/a	3.63	n/a	n/a	n/a	5.47	n/a	n/a	n/a	n/a

MEAN NUMBER OF DAYS WITH 0.01 INCH OR MORE OF PRECIPITATION

	Jan.	Feb.	Mar.	Apr.	May	June	July	Aug.	Sep.	Oct.	Nov.	Dec.
Asheville	10	9	11	9	12	11	12	12	9	8	9	10
Boone*	9	7	9	8	8	9	11	9	7	5	6	7
Roanoke	10	10	11	10	12	10	12	11	8	8	9	9

(* 0.1 inch or more)

Camping versus Lodging

If you are considering an extended tour of the Skyline Drive and the Parkway, the first decision you will probably make is whether to camp or stay in motels. There are pros and cons to both approaches. However, if you can afford motels, your trip will be easier and more comfortable. Without sleeping bag, pad, tent, and cooking gear, you can make better time on the road. Credit-card touring is definitely the streamlined way to go.

Many lodges along the Skyline Drive and Parkway are memorable for their high ceilings and exposed beams, large stone fireplaces, decks and porches for lounging, and restaurants featuring southern mountain cooking. From people-watching by the fireplace in the great room at Big Meadows to gazing out at cow pastures on the deck at Bluffs Lodge, lodges heighten the rustic mountain experience.

There are five lodges within strict Park Service boundaries of the Skyline Drive and the Parkway. Although Skyland Lodge and Big Meadows Lodge are spaced nicely along the Skyline Drive, the lodges along the Parkway are far apart. Peaks of Otter Lodge is 150 miles from Bluffs Lodge at Doughton Park. After that, the only other Park Service lodge is at Mount Pisgah. In Part Two of the book, we outline all Park Service and private facilities along these roads.

We have devised a rating system for the cost of motels and lodges. These rates are subject to change, particularly during special events and during the leaf season. Please call ahead.

$	inexpensive	up to $50
$$	moderate	$51–$80
$$$	expensive	$81 and up

Private concessionaires operate all of the restaurants and lodges along the Skyline Drive and the Parkway. There are no other businesses within the boundaries of either park. Essentially, the Blue Ridge Parkway boundaries are very narrow as the road winds through the Blue Ridge. The major facilities along the Parkway include: Otter Creek, Peaks of Otter, Roanoke Mountain, Rocky Knob, Mabry Mill, Cumberland Knob, Doughton Park, Moses H. Cone, Julian Price Memorial Park, Linville Falls, Crabtree Meadows, Craggy Gardens, and Mount Pisgah. The Skyline Drive differs because it is surrounded by the much larger Shenandoah National Park. While the Park Service maintains facilities at Matthews Arm, Skyland, Big Meadows, Lewis Mountain, and Loft Mountain, the surrounding areas along the Skyline Drive are protected as national parklands.

Because the Parkway has so few facilities within its boundaries in proportion to its length, we have provided information on motels and campgrounds off of the Parkway. When you study the Parkway map, you see that it is feasible to tour from one Park Service campground to another. There are some long, difficult stretches between these campgrounds. It is 70 miles from Rocky Knob campground to Doughton Park campground; 65 miles from Doughton Park to the next Park Service campground at Julian Price. That may be more than you want to cover in a day. And if it rains or fog sets in, what then? That's why you need

The Inn at Glendale Springs lends quaint charm to this community.

alternatives when touring the Parkway. Things hardly ever go according to plan.

Park Service campgrounds are distinctive in several ways. They are all situated within large tracts of Park Service land ranging in size from 250 acres to 7,000 acres. Most of these campgrounds are fairly secluded in wooded areas. Like the lodges, each campground has a charm all its own. Otter Creek has its namesake flowing alongside campsites; Peaks of Otter and Julian Price are situated beside lakes; deer roam freely throughout Big Meadows; and you pitch your tent amidst gnarled, ancient balsams at Mount Pisgah. Big Meadows on the Skyline Drive is the largest campground with 217 sites. The smallest, Lewis Mountain Campground, has 32 sites and is also on the Skyline Drive.

The big difference between the Skyline Drive and the Parkway campgrounds is that nearly all Skyline Drive campgrounds have pay showers (the exception is Matthews Arm). There are absolutely no showers in Blue Ridge Parkway campgrounds. Shenandoah National Park (Skyline Drive) has more conveniences than the Parkway. The camp stores are much more elaborate. The campgrounds along the Skyline Drive have laundry facilities. Although there are several private campgrounds along the Parkway with shower and laundry facilities, none of the Park Service campgrounds on the Parkway have either convenience. Most likely, backpackers on the Appalachian Trail are the reason for these amenities on the Skyline Drive. With the Appalachian Trail running through Shenandoah National Park and paralleling the Skyline Drive, Park Service facilities are the primary source for hikers. The Appalachian Trail intersects the Parkway at a few points, but these intersections are not near Park Service facilities.

The physical layout of the typical campground in both parks is very similar. Paved roads run through the campgrounds. Tents and RVs have separate areas. Each tent site has a groomed tent pad, picnic table, and grill. Within clustered sites you will find running water, rest rooms, and trash receptacles. Some campgrounds have bear poles if the campground is located in "bear country." All campgrounds have an amphitheater or gathering place, pay telephones, and rangers on duty.

Daily rates for Skyline Drive campgrounds are $14 per site ($17 per site at Big Meadows after May 13). The Parkway charges

Blue Ridge Country is the only American Youth Hostel on the Parkway.

$12–$20 per site in all campgrounds except Dundo. All camp-grounds are filled on a first-come, first-served basis except Big Meadows and Dundo Campground, which require reservations. Dundo is a primitive group campground primarily used for scout-ing and educational purposes. The sites can accommodate from 8 to 20 campers and are $32 per site. Call (800) 365-CAMP to place a reservation. Big Meadows remains open through November; the other campgrounds in the park close October 31.

We think camping is a great experience in and of itself. Although it does require more effort in the long run, combining camping with lodging allows you the best of both worlds. A fully loaded touring bike gives you all the options. If you decide you can go no farther, but there is nothing civilized for miles, you can pull off the road and have a tent over your head and the means to cook a decent meal. With credit-card touring you must plan ahead. If you are not capable of covering the mileage to make your motel reservation there is little to fall back on.

The best way to decide which approach to bicycle touring suits you is to weigh the pros and cons. We figure it can't hurt to spell them all out.

CAMPING

Advantages of Camping:

- Camping is less expensive.
- Camping is an experience in and of itself.
- There is a tendency to meet more people. Campers seem to open up to the novelty of the touring cyclist.
- You have more options. With facilities sometimes far apart, it is a plus to have both camping and lodging possibilities.

Disadvantages of Camping:

- The extra gear required increases the weight you must carry.
- Housekeeping chores, such as setting up and breaking camp, require more time.
- There are no showers in Parkway campgrounds.

◆ You must be prepared for inclement weather.

◆ During peak times, some campgrounds fill up. The campgrounds on the Skyline Drive reach capacity more often than
those on the Parkway. It can be impossible to obtain sites at
peak times. If camping at Big Meadows on the Skyline Drive,
you must make reservations ahead of time (see page 49).

◆ Only two Park Service campgrounds are open in the winter
months: Otter Creek in Virginia (Milepost 60) and Linville Falls
in North Carolina (Milepost 316). Park Service campgrounds
open between early April and mid-May and close around
October 31 (except for Big Meadows, Otter Creek, and Linville
Falls; see above).

LODGING

Advantages of Lodging:

◆ Spending your nights in motels allows streamlined, efficient
touring: no sleeping bags, tents, cooking gear, etc.

◆ With less weight you can tour faster and cover more miles
each day.

◆ There are some wonderful lodges along the Skyline Drive and
the Parkway.

◆ You can expect the creature comforts of home: showers, a
warm, dry bed; a TV; etc.

Disadvantages of Lodging:

◆ Reservations are advisable and, at peak times, required.

◆ Most motels have required check-in times. If you fail to arrive
on time at your destination, you may lose your room. Usually,
you can guarantee a room with a major credit card.

◆ Motels and lodges are open seasonally. Generally, this is
May 1 through October 31.

◆ Rates are subject to change.

Gearing Up: Special Equipment and Clothing

When making choices on equipment and clothing for bicycling in the mountains, three tenets should be foremost in your mind:

- ◆ know your abilities
- ◆ know your bicycle
- ◆ anticipate the weather

Everything we say here may seem obvious, but we want to emphasize the key issues.

BICYCLES AND TOOLS

With the many choices of high-tech bicycles and cycling equipment on the market, we suggest that you select the best you can afford. If you cannot purchase everything you need all at once, upgrade later. We highly recommend using sealed components as much as possible: sealed headsets, bottom brackets, hubs, and pedals. In the long run, sealed components will endure, especially through adverse weather conditions.

While we choose not to discuss gear ratios, we advise you to make an honest assessment of your abilities when setting your bike up for mountain cycling. The Assault on Mount Mitchell, a 102-mile endurance event, is an extreme case, but it is a classic example of bicyclists getting in over their heads. Each year that we participate, we see a steady procession of cyclists reduced to walking their bikes along the Parkway and the five miles up to the summit of Mount Mitchell. This is not the sad fate of one or two cyclists; what you see is 30 or 40 people who thought they would be able to cycle through exhaustion with the gearing they had selected. For more information on the Assault on Mount Mitchell, see the descriptive section on page 109.

If you are considering an extended trip of the Parkway and the Skyline Drive, and you have never toured in mountainous terrain, a triple crankset is a must. Fully loaded panniers make a difference in any terrain. Mountains truly magnify any weight you choose to carry. We have toured thousands of miles with conventional shifting mechanisms that work quite well. However, index-shifting systems are ideal for mountain cycling.

Having the right tool for the right emergency is not always possible. You should carry the bare essentials on every ride. There are so few bike shops along the Skyline Drive and the Parkway that you really need to put some thought into tool selection. If you are day tripping, it is a good idea to have at least a comprehensive selection of tools in your car and a basic tool kit on your bike. If you are making an extended tour, you want to strike a balance. The weight of tools can really add up, but a bike emergency can leave you stranded. In some situations you may have to hitch a ride to the nearest bike shop. See Appendix A for a list of the bike shops within a reasonable distance of the Parkway.

If you need help selecting tools and equipment for your bike, we suggest you take your bike to your local shop and ask a mechanic for advice. All good bike shops are more than happy to spend time showing you how to use the proper tools to make minor adjustments on your bike. Of course, any time you cycle on the Parkway you should make sure your bike is in top condition.

One investment you might consider is quality wheels. Hand-built wheels with sealed hubs should spare you much aggravation. In any event, tools you will want on hand if you are touring are a spoke wrench and spare spokes.

We have compiled a list of the tools we think are absolutely essential. Most of these tools will fit in the type of bag that mounts under a bicycle saddle. If you are making day trips, you can leave off the spokes, cables, and spare tire.

CHARLIE'S LIST OF ESSENTIAL TOOLS:

- chain breaker
- spoke wrench
- spare spokes
- pliers
- small adjustable wrench
- allen wrenches
- tire levers
- brake cable (front and rear)
- derailleur cable (front and rear)
- spare tire, tubes, and patch kit
- multipurpose lubricant
- air pump (which attaches to bike frame)

Make sure your air pump works properly and has the correct head for the type of tube you use, Presta or Schrader. Just remember, on the Parkway and the Skyline Drive proper, there is practically zero availability of bicycle parts. A rudimentary knowledge of bicycle repair is a required bicycle skill.

If you have absolutely no mechanical aptitude, you might want to carry a small repair manual that can guide you through basic repairs. After all, compared to most machines, a bicycle is not that complicated. We recommend the following titles:

Linnard Zinn, *Zinn and the Art of Road Bike Maintenence* (Velo Press, 2000).

Rob Van der Plas, *Road Bike Maintenance* (Van der Plas Publications, 1996).

Jim Langley, *Bicycling Magazine's Complete Guide to Bicycle Maintenance and Repair for Road and Mountain Bikes* (Rodale Press, 1999).

CLOTHING

Certain clothing items are essential, even for weekend trips in the Blue Ridge. Needless to say, weather should govern all the clothing choices you make. We highly recommend a GORE-TEX® rainsuit. In our opinion, this item above all others is the most essential for

Any time you cycle on the Parkway, you should make sure your bike is in top condition.

cycling in the Blue Ridge. At the very minimum, a windbreaker or some water-repellent jacket is a must. This is necessary not only for rain but for sudden cold temperatures and windy conditions as well.

Is GORE-TEX® fabric really worth it? We think so. We cycled in the rain with regular nylon rainsuits for years and got by. As you may know, GORE-TEX® is great because it breathes. It does an excellent job of keeping water out, yet when your body heats up, you perspire less because air is able to circulate underneath the fabric. GORE-TEX® is not perfect, but it is a vast improvement over other fabrics.

You might think that in the summer months you won't need a rainsuit or a jacket. Our experience has shown us otherwise. We have been caught in downpours on the Parkway with no choice but to will away the chill from a body-drenching rain. If nothing else, a rainsuit or jacket will help keep you warm.

In spring and fall, the temperature can fluctuate quite a bit. Chilly temperatures make tights or leg warmers a good idea. A synthetic top is a good item to have on hand, even in the summer, for sudden drops in temperature. You should keep in mind that the mountains can be chilly even at the height of summer. Other than these few specifics, let personal taste dictate your choices.

One common mistake for touring cyclists is to pack too much stuff. You may not need as much clothing as you think. If you do laundry along the way, you should be able to get by with less.

ZIPLOC BAGS

While we're on the subject of packing gear, we would like to sing the praises of one magic item, Ziploc bags. This simple household item is indispensable for keeping your gear dry. Panniers, and other bicycle bags, are not entirely waterproof. In a downpour, Ziploc bags will save you from a soggy mess. They also force you to pack more scientifically, since even the gallon-sized bags will only hold so much.

Weather should govern all the clothing choices you make.

HELMETS

It is a grave mistake not to wear a helmet when bicycling. There is no valid reason for not wearing one. We sincerely urge you to wear a helmet at all times while cycling and to wear it properly—not cocked back away from your forehead or unfastened.

LIGHTING SYSTEMS

Due to the frequency of rain, fog, and tunnels on these highways, the Park Service requires some type of lighting system. Front and rear lights could save your life. Not only do lighting systems make you more visible to cars in inclement weather, they help you find your way through the longer tunnels. Some of the tunnels you will encounter are long enough, or curved enough, to leave you in total darkness. Not only can cars inflict injury, you can easily hurt yourself by taking a spill on a rock or running into the wall of a tunnel.

We use a flashing belt beacon for the rear of our bikes and a white light for the front. Generator- and battery-operated lights each have advantages. Carrying extra bulbs and batteries is a good idea as some of the smaller bike shops do not stock every type of bulb.

THE CHECKLIST

Finally, we provide you with a master list of the things you should think about taking for the long haul. If you are going out on weekend trips, you can obviously omit some things. We have learned the hard way about carrying too much gear on a bicycle. In 1985, we cycled halfway across the country before we learned how to pack efficiently. To our relief, we finally had it right when we toured the Skyline Drive. We cycled from Front Royal to Asheville without a wobble. If you can get by with less, do it.

What to Bring for an Extended Tour of the Blue Ridge:

◆ cycling shorts, two pairs
◆ T-shirts or cycling jerseys, three
◆ thermal underwear (Capilene®, CoolMax®, or something similar), one
◆ running shorts, one pair
◆ shorts, one pair
◆ GORE-TEX® rainsuit
◆ lightweight wind jacket
◆ swimsuit
◆ socks, underwear, etc.
◆ cycling gloves
◆ cycling hat, optional
◆ cycling helmet, highly recommended
◆ cycling shoes

What to Bring *(continued)*

- shoes, alternate pair
- sandals or flip-flops, optional
- towel, one (as lightweight as you can find)
- toiletries
- first-aid kit
- wristwatch
- sunglasses
- sunscreen
- camera and film
- notepad, pens, stamps, etc.
- flashlight, small
- cookstove, fuel, and matches
- mess kit (don't forget the can opener)
- rope (a multipurpose item)
- lightweight sleeping bag and pad
- tent and ground cloth

PART 2:
POINT-BY-POINT
DESCRIPTIONS

THE SKYLINE DRIVE AND BLUE RIDGE PARKWAY

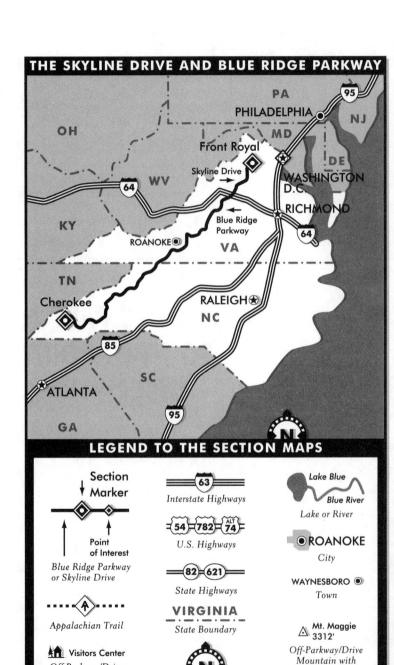

LEGEND TO THE SECTION MAPS

↓ Section
Marker

◆◎◆

↑ Point
of Interest
Blue Ridge Parkway
or Skyline Drive

•••••Ⓐ•••••
Appalachian Trail

🏚 Visitors Center
Off-Parkway/Drive
Point of Interest

═══（63）═══
Interstate Highways

═（54）（782）（74ᴬᴸᵀ）═
U.S. Highways

═（82）（621）═
State Highways

VIRGINIA
State Boundary

Ⓝ
Compass Rose

Lake Blue
Blue River
Lake or River

◉ROANOKE
City

WAYNESBORO ◉
Town

△ Mt. Maggie
3312'
Off-Parkway/Drive
Mountain with
Height in Feet

An Explanation of Our Point-by-Point Descriptions

In our point-by-point breakdown of the Skyline Drive and the Parkway, we list motels, lodges, restaurants, grocery stores, and campgrounds on and off of these roads. We also list area hospitals and any bicycle shops within a reasonable distance. Bicycle shops are not in abundance. Because of this, we also list hardware stores that might help you out of a jam.

Our criteria for including facilities off of these roads take several factors into account. We have not ventured more than five miles off these roads with the exception of a few towns we choose to highlight. In most cases, we have not included facilities more than one to three miles off the road. We have investigated all side roads except those that are strictly residential. We do not recommend roads that involve extreme descents unless there is something on that road to justify an arduous climb back up.

We have not rated the quality of facilities, although we do make remarks about those that made a favorable impression upon us.

We begin at Milepost 0 on the Skyline Drive and travel south. If you decide to travel north just work backwards from specific mileposts. Generally, we divide our sections by Park Service facilities. In some cases, a town will be the dividing point.

There are as many approaches to bicycling in the Blue Ridge as there are riders. A strong rider with gear could reasonably tour the Skyline Drive in two days. Unencumbered by gear, one could cycle the Skyline Drive in a single day. Then again, there are so many things to see along the way, and so many trails to hike, that spending a week there would not be unreasonable.

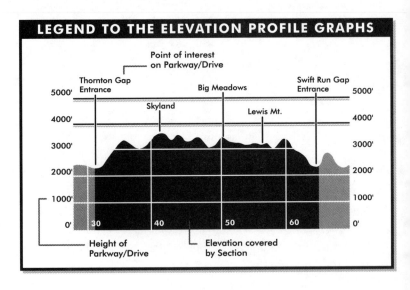

The Skyline Drive

The Skyline Drive is a scenic highway that runs the length of Shenandoah National Park for a total of 105.5 miles. Shenandoah National Park (hereafter referred to as "the Park") is comprised of 195,000 acres near George Washington and Jefferson National Forests in western Virginia. Not only does the scenic highway dissect the Park, but 95 miles of the Appalachian Trail are within park boundaries.

As you cycle along the Skyline Drive, the Shenandoah Valley runs parallel to the west, while the Piedmont extends eastward toward the coast. Small details in the construction of the Skyline Drive give it a slightly different atmosphere from the Blue Ridge Parkway. Stone and mortar walls grace the edge of the road as it winds along the Blue Ridge Mountains. These structures and the tendency of the trees to form a canopy over the road give the Skyline Drive a secluded feeling.

Since the Skyline Drive runs continuously through national forest lands, wildlife may be more prevalent here than along the

Parkway. There is a large Virginia white-tailed deer population in the Park. You are guaranteed to spot deer at dawn or dusk. Black bear also inhabit the Park. Bear sightings have become more frequent over the years, as evidenced by the bearproof trashcans and bear poles found at campgrounds and picnic areas. Other wildlife includes the red fox, the gray fox, the striped skunk, the spotted skunk, the bobcat, the raccoon, the beaver, the groundhog, and the chipmunk. There are about 200 species of birds in the Park. Among the larger birds in the Park, you will find the wild turkey, the raven, and the ruffed grouse.

Trees in the George Washington National Forest are primarily young second growth as a result of heavy timbering practiced before the park was established. The primary species include oak and hickory, but you will also find black locust, hemlock, yellow birch, black birch, basswood, tulip poplar, red maple, and sugar maple.

If bicycle touring in the mountains is a new experience for you, the Skyline Drive is a good place to start. Facilities abound, with 25 miles being the largest gap between a source of food and

Elizabeth enjoys a moment to read.

the highway. There are two lodges, six restaurants, four camp stores, and four campgrounds in the space of 105 miles. In addition, all but one of the campgrounds have showers. That is pretty good, especially when compared to those along the Parkway. Since this is a national park, there is an entry fee of $5 fee, good for seven consecutive days.

Now that you have provided your basic needs, you are free to concentrate on some very pleasant bicycling. The grades on the Skyline Drive are not as severe as they are on the Parkway. The longest climbs and descents are at the northern and southern entrances. The elevation drops to 1,390 feet at the Front Royal entrance and 1,900 feet at the Rockfish Gap entrance near Waynesboro.

FRONT ROYAL TO THORNTON GAP [0–31.5]

Front Royal, Virginia, is one of the most popular starting points for extended tours of the Blue Ridge. The closest airports to Front Royal are approximately 70 miles away in Washington, D.C. You can cycle out of either Dulles International Airport or Washington National Airport to Front Royal.

When you enter Shenandoah National Park on a bicycle, you experience the sensation of being transported into a separate world. At the height of the summer the vegetation is thick and alive with secrets, as if you were traveling through an enchanted forest. The deeper you go the more entranced you become. Kudzu climbs greedily in the lower elevations. On hot days there is steamy humidity. Slowly, you climb from Front Royal to the higher elevations.

The fact is you have to do some work to reach the Blue Ridge proper. The first ten miles of the Skyline Drive climb Dickey Ridge before connecting with the Blue Ridge mountain range at Compton Gap (Milepost 10.4). You climb nearly 2,800 feet in this 22-mile stretch up to 3,385 feet at Hogback Overlook.

There are numerous overlooks in this section. At most of these overlooks the Shenandoah River is visible. Take note of the Massanutten Ridge, which divides the Shenandoah Valley for nearly 50 miles. When you study the rock along the Skyline Drive, you are looking at molten lava flows called the Catoctin formation.

Matthews Arm is the first campground on the Skyline Drive as you travel south. There is no food here, but Elkwallow Wayside is just two miles south with a restaurant and camp store. There are three hikes, which originate from the campground: Traces Trail, Knob Mountain, and Overall Run Falls. From Matthews Arm, you travel another 10 miles, dipping down to 2,304 feet at the Thornton Gap Entrance Station.

Milepost

00.0   Front Royal, Virginia (elevation 590 feet)

Front Royal is situated at the north entrance of the Skyline Drive. Facilities include a post office, hospital, numerous restaurants, and motels—but no bicycle shop. The closest "pro" shop is 18 miles away in Winchester (see appendix). All lodging mention below is reached by turning right off of Skyline Drive and driving north on US 340.

**Woodward House on Manor Grade
(800) 635-7011, (540) 635-7010;
www.acountryhome.com $$$**
Located at 413 South Royal Avenue, three blocks north from the Skyline Drive at US 340 and US 55.

**Chester House Bed & Breakfast
(540) 635-3937; www.chesterhouse.com $$$**
Located at 43 Chester Street. Turn right onto Main Street, then left onto Chester Street.

Center City Motel (540) 635-4050 $

Scottish Inn (540) 636-6168 $–$$

Pioneer Motel (540) 635-4784 $
Located at 541 S Royal Avenue, just one block north from the Skyline Drive.

Shenandoah Motel (540) 635-3181 $
Located 2.5 miles north on US 340 on 1600 North Shenandoah Avenue.

04.6 Dickey Ridge Visitor Center (elevation 1,940 feet)

The information center has a ranger on duty to answer questions. This facility includes exhibits, a gift shop, water, rest rooms, a picnic area, and a nature trail. There is no camping or food here. Open mid-April–August.

21.0 Hogback Overlook (elevation 3,385 feet)

This is the highest point so far. Hogback Overlook affords excellent views of the Shenandoah Valley and Shenandoah River.

22.2 Matthews Arm (elevation 2,750 feet)

A steep, 0.8-mile descent leads to the most primitive campground on the Skyline Drive; there are no showers or laundry facilities. If you need supplies, the Elkwallow

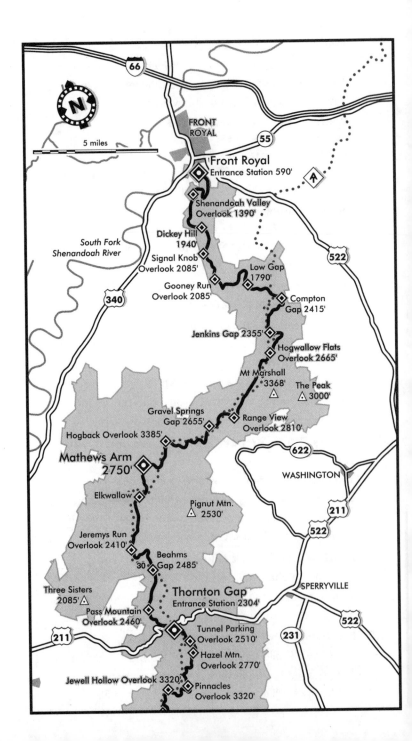

Wayside lies 2 miles south. There are 179 campsites here each $16 per night, open mid-May–October

24.1 Elkwallow Wayside and Picnic Area

There's a grill that serves breakfast and other simple fare, a gift shop, and a store with groceries and camping supplies. Open April–August. A water and comfort station is available in the picnic area. The trail to Jeremy's Run, one of the major trout streams in the park, originates here.

31.5 Thornton Gap (elevation 2,304 feet) US 211/522

Panorama

This former restaurant is now a gift shop. Rest rooms and water are available. You can view Marys Rock from the deck.

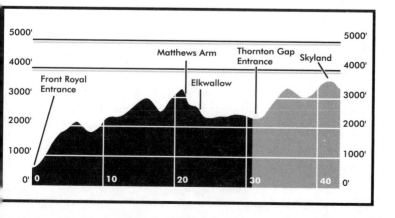

THORNTON GAP TO SWIFT RUN GAP [31.5–65.5]

The numerous overlooks and hiking trails highlighting streams, waterfalls, and geologic formations are good reasons for taking your time along the Skyline Drive. At Thornton Gap you can view Marys Rock, which is formed of granodiorite. Marys Rock Tunnel, just south of Thornton Gap, is the only tunnel on the Skyline Drive. As you make your way south toward Skyland Lodge, views of Pinnacles and the profile of Stony Man Mountain dominate the area.

South of Skyland, as you approach the highest point on Skyline Drive (elevation 3,680 feet), Hawksbill Mountain dominates the skyline as the highest peak in Shenandoah National Park (elevation 4,051 feet). The Franklin Cliffs Overlook between Mileposts 49 and 50 has great rocky cliffs, perfect for a siesta on a sunny day. If you have time for an hour's hike, Dark Hollow Falls is a good choice at Milepost 50.7, just north of Big Meadows.

The trailhead to Bearfence Mountain summit is found at Milepost 56.4. The hike is a little less than a mile round-trip for a 360-degree view of the area. From this rocky summit you can see Massanutten Ridge, Shenandoah Valley, Grindstone, Green, Powell, and Smith Mountains to the west. To the east, there are a dozen peaks within view—Hazeltop, Bush Mountain, Laurel Gap, and Buzzard Rocks are among them. This hike is only a mile from Lewis Mountain. You might want to drop your gear, set up camp, and cycle back for a hike.

Another reason for taking your time: visiting the park's two lodges—Skyland and Big Meadows. While there are plenty of camping possibilities on this section, you may want to consider spending a night at one or both of these lodges. Both are spectacular places to lay your head. If you choose not to spend the night at Skyland, consider having lunch there. The dining room at Skyland is filled with windows perfect for gazing at the Shenandoah Valley. When we think of Big Meadows, the other lodge, two things

immediately come to mind: blueberries and deer. Deer sightings
are possible at all times of the day. At dawn and dusk, the
meadow directly across from the visitor center attracts anywhere
from 10 to 50 grazing deer. Take note that the meadow is filled
with blueberries ripe for picking in July and August.

Big Meadows is the most extensive facility on the Skyline
Drive. The campground here uses a reservation system, and reservations are required starting May 14 until it closes at the end of
November; call (800) 365-CAMP up to three months in advance.
Big Meadows Lodge has a cozy, rustic charm. We spent two memorable days fogged and rained in here one September. The dining
room and great room of the lodge have high ceilings with
exposed beams and wrought-iron ceiling fixtures. The massive

Small farms stretch
across the Shenan-
doah Valley below.

stone fireplace in the great room has a magnetic force on foul-weather days.

Big Meadows is a major stop for hikers on the Appalachian Trail. The camp store here is superbly stocked. Food items have been selected in sizes and types suitable for campers. The camp store sells clothing, such as parkas and jeans; and supplies, such as candles, Coleman fuel, and toiletries. Big Meadows is the halfway point on the Skyline Drive. A strong rider could easily cover the Skyline Drive in two days with Big Meadows being the logical overnight stop.

If you plan on camping at the halfway point on the Skyline Drive, Lewis Mountain is a good alternative to Big Meadows. Lewis Mountain campground has fewer campsites than Big Meadows, but the atmosphere is less hectic, without the constant flow of traffic the larger complex attracts. There are also a few housekeeping cabins here, which require a reservation.

If you are heading south, you have a great 1,000-foot descent to Swift Run Gap, one of four entrance stations on the Skyline Drive.

Milepost

32.2 Marys Rock Tunnel (670 feet)

This is the only tunnel in Shenandoah National Park, and one of only two in Virginia.

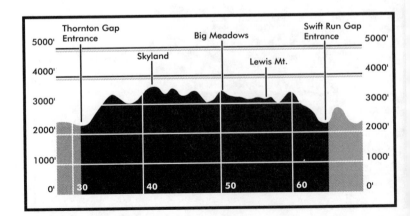

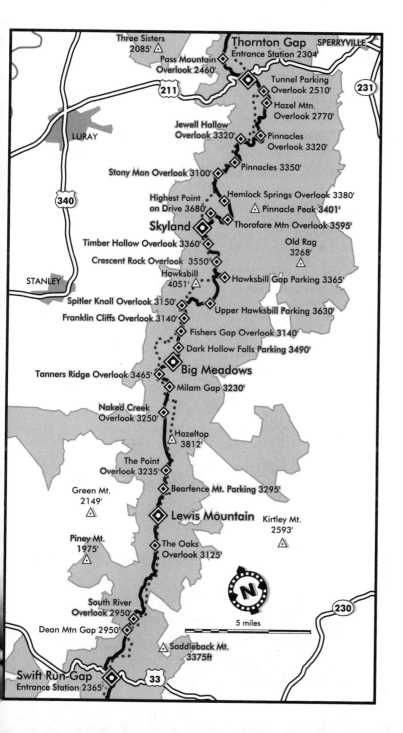

36.7 Pinnacles

This picnic area is a point of access to the Appalachian Trail. Rustic rest rooms and water are available.

41.7 Entrance to Skyland Lodge (elevation 3,680 feet)

Skyland Lodge (540) 999-2211; (800) 999-4714 $$–$$$

It's a 0.5-mile ride to Skyland's lodge, cabins, restaurant, tap room, and gift shop. There is no camping here.

Open April–November

46.7 Upper Hawksbill Parking Area (elevation 3,630 feet)

Hawksbill Mountain (elevation 4,051 feet) is the highest point within park boundaries. The trail to the summit is 2 miles round-trip.

50.7 Dark Hollow Falls (elevation 3,425 feet)

The trail to the falls is 1.5 miles round-trip.

51.0 Big Meadows

Harry F. Byrd, Sr. Visitor Center
Exhibits on history and development of Skyline Drive. While rest rooms and water are available year-round, the visitor center is open April–August.

Big Meadows Lodge (540) 999-2221 $$–$$$

A 1.1-mile road leads to a rustic lodge, cabins, dining facilities, tap room, and gift shop. Big Meadows has a campground with showers, laundry facilities, and an excellent camp store. The campground has 217 sites. The visitor center conducts a variety of naturalist's programs each day. Campground rates are $19 per night; open April–November. For reservations call (800) 365-CAMP or go to www.reservations.nps.gov.

56.4 Bearfence Mountain Parking Area

The hike to the summit is only 0.8 mile round-trip.

57.5 **Lewis Mountain (elevation 3,390 feet)**
(540) 999-2255, (800) 999-4714 $$ (cabins)
You will find complete facilities here including a camp-
ground, housekeeping cabins, showers, laundry facilities,
and a camp store (open May–August). This camp store
has food and camping equipment on half the scale of the
Big Meadows store. Lewis Mountain has 32 campsites.
Rates are $16 per night and open early spring–October.

62.6 **South River Picnic Area**

65.5 **Swift Run Gap (elevation 2,365 feet) – US 33**
Town of Elkton lies to the west. The elevation difference
between gap and town is 1,400 feet.

Two cyclists stop to confer with their map just before reaching Skyland Lodge.

SWIFT RUN GAP TO ROCKFISH GAP [65.5–105.5]

From Swift Run Gap southward, there is a mixed bag of up and down, but the road ultimately climbs into the Loft Mountain area. Loft Mountain Wayside is directly off the Skyline Drive. However, the road to the campground is an uphill challenge. If Loft Mountain campground is your destination for the day, save some energy for the climb to the top.

Loft Mountain campground has some outstanding campsites. It is worth dragging your bike down into one of the more secluded wooded sites. Deer wander freely through these areas. The Appalachian Trail is no more than 100 yards from one side of the campground; it's great to have just beyond your tent. You can hike a stretch and ponder the differences between experiencing the Blue Ridge by foot and by bicycle.

From Loft Mountain, it is 25 miles to the end of the Skyline Drive and the beginning of the Blue Ridge Parkway. If you are heading south, you have an easy descent into Rockfish Gap. If you are heading north toward Loft Mountain, you can expect a steady climb much of the way (nearly a 1,000-foot gain).

For travelers doing a long-distance tour of the Skyline Drive and the Parkway, Waynesboro is a good overnight stop. With medical facilities and the full range of shopping opportunities, Waynesboro is one of the few cities in close proximity to the Skyline Drive and the Parkway—about four miles west of Rockfish Gap. The only disadvantage of a stopover in Waynesboro is that you will start out with a four-mile climb from the town proper back up to the Skyline Drive. Fortunately, if lodging and food are all you require, there are two motels just off the Skyline Drive at Rockfish Gap.

Northbounders who need the services of a bike shop should take advantage of the ones here; the next accessible bike shop is past the end of the Skyline Drive in Winchester, about 120 miles away. For southbounders, the next shop is 50 miles away in Lexington.

Milepost

79.5 Loft Mountain

Loft Mountain Wayside

The wayside has an information area, gift shop, comfort station, water, and grill, which serves breakfast and lunch fare. Open late-May–August.

Loft Mountain Campground   (434) 823-4675

There is a steep, one-mile climb to the campground. The adjoining campstore is well-stocked with camp gear and groceries. Showers and laundry facilities make this a good stop for those doing extended tours. If you're heading south, this is your last chance for shower and laundry facilities in a National Park Service campground. Loft Mountain has 219 campsites. Rates are $16 per night and open early-May–October.

105.4 Rockfish Gap (elevation 1,909 feet) – US 250

Rockfish Gap marks the end of the Skyline Drive. After this, the road becomes the Blue Ridge Parkway. Exit here for Waynesboro. Take US 250 West four miles into Waynesboro, which has a post office, hospital, lodging, restaurants, and two bicycle shops. There are two motels at Rockfish Gap, which should spare a descent into town.

Inn at Afton   US 250 East, Waynesboro; (540) 942-5201 $$

Located on west side. After exiting parkway, take immediate left up VA 601. An attached restaurant offers breakfast, lunch, and dinner.

Colony House Motel   (540) 942-4156 $–$$

This popular stop for hikers as well as cyclists is located 0.8 miles west on US 250. Continental breakfast is included. Has pool and laundry facilities. Local restaurants offer free delivery.

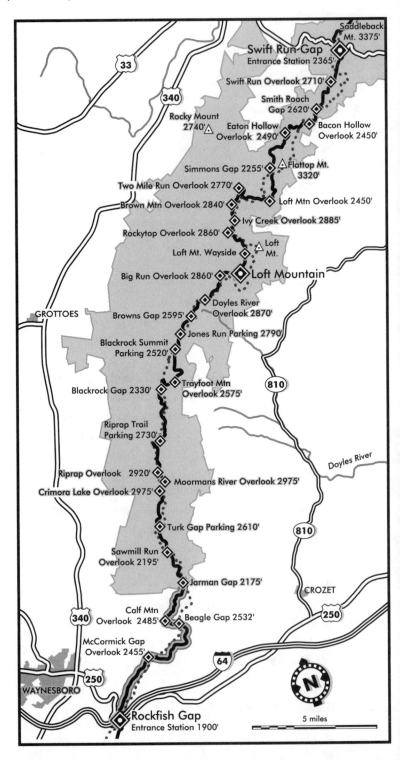

Saddleback
Mt. 3375'

Swift Run Gap
Entrance Station 2365'

Swift Run Overlook 2710'

Smith Roach
Gap 2620'

Rocky Mount
2740'

Eaton Hollow
Overlook 2490'

Bacon Hollow
Overlook 2450'

Simmons Gap 2255'

Flattop Mt.
3320'

Two Mile Run Overlook 2770'

Brown Mtn Overlook 2840'

Loft Mtn Overlook 2450'

Ivy Creek Overlook 2885'

Rockytop Overlook 2860'

Loft
Mt.

Loft Mt. Wayside

Big Run Overlook 2860'

Loft Mountain

GROTTOES

Doyles River
Overlook 2870'

Browns Gap 2595'

Jones Run Parking 2790'

Blackrock Summit
Parking 2520'

Trayfoot Mtn
Overlook 2575'

Blackrock Gap 2330'

810

Riprap Trail
Parking 2730'

Riprap Overlook   2920'

Moormans River Overlook 2975'

Crimora Lake Overlook 2975'

Doyles River

Turk Gap Parking 2610'

810

Sawmill Run
Overlook 2195'

Jarman Gap 2175'

CROZET

Calf Mtn
Overlook 2485'

Beagle Gap 2532'

340

McCormick Gap
Overlook 2455'

250

64

250

N

WAYNESBORO

Rockfish Gap
Entrance Station 1900'

5 miles

**Rockfish Gap Outfitters   1461 East Main Street,
Waynesboro; (540) 943-1461**
This bicycle and outdoors shop is located three miles west
on US 250 heading into town. Hours: Monday–Saturday,
10 a.m.–6 p.m.

**Cycle-Recycle Company   (540) 949-8973;
www.cyclerecycle.com**
Located six miles from the Parkway. Take US 250, which
turns into Main Street. Located in downtown Waynesboro
at 320 West Main Street. Hours: Monday–Saturday,
9 a.m.–6 p.m.

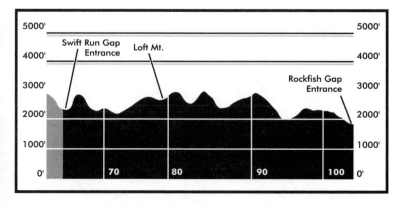

The Blue Ridge Parkway

With little fanfare, the Blue Ridge Parkway begins at Rockfish Gap and continues south for 470 miles. The mile markers still mark the terminus of the Parkway as 469 miles even though the construction of the Linn Cove Viaduct added an extra mile. Whereas the Skyline Drive is enclosed by national forests, the Parkway winds its way through some disparate geographic situations. The Parkway skirts around two fairly large cities, Roanoke and Asheville. Yet, the Parkway does take you through rugged wilderness areas, such as Shining Rock, Linville Gorge, and Pisgah National Forest. Any single-day trip by bicycle along the Parkway can leave you with distinctly different impressions. One day you roll past cabbage patches and rust-colored barns; the next day your surroundings are craggy, rocky, and downright mountainous.

When you're speeding down the side of a mountain, it's easy to experience sensory overload. Greens blur, the wind roars in your ears, and your adrenaline rises with a rush of feeling. The numerous, inevitable ascents of the Parkway, whether they be a quarter-mile or six miles long, are the best times to take note of the flowers, animals, rocks, and trees that surround you.

Once again, trees dominate the natural scene in the Blue Ridge. In his book, *A Naturalist's Blue Ridge Parkway*, David Catlin devotes an entire chapter to the integral role trees play. He explains:

It is difficult to overstate the importance of trees in the natural history of the mountains, for trees greatly determine not only the kinds, but the character of life here. It can even be legitimately claimed that trees put the 'Blue' in Blue Ridge, for hydrocarbons released into the atmosphere by the forest contribute to the characteristic haze on these mountains and to their distinctive color.

There are many distinct forests in the Blue Ridge. In the lower elevations there are oak-chestnut, cove hardwood, and oak-pine forests. The oak-chestnut forests are primarily white, northern red, black, scarlet, and chestnut oaks. The chestnut tree was once prominent along the Blue Ridge, but the chestnut blight fungus wiped out these valuable trees around the turn of the century.

Cove hardwood forests thrive in damp soils. These also feature tulip trees, sugar maple, yellow buckeye, basswood, beech, yellow birch, northern red oak, and black cherry. Areas with good examples of cove hardwood forests include the James River Visitor Center and, closer to the Smokies, Standing Rock Overlook and Big Witch Tunnel.

Oak-pine forests exist in dryer, sandier soils, especially around the Asheville area. Species of southern Appalachian pines include white pine, shortleaf pine, pitch pine, Virginia pine, and Table Mountain pine.

In the higher elevations of 5,000 feet or more are northern hardwoods and spruce-fir forests. The northern hardwoods include trees found in the woods of Pennsylvania, New York, and New England. Beech, yellow buckeye, and yellow birch are all found.

The areas with spruce-fir forests are among the most memorable along the Parkway. Found in the very highest elevations, red spruce and Fraser fir are the distinctive inhabitants of Mount Mitchell, Richland Balsam, and Waterrock Knob. Unfortunately, environmental stresses, both man-made and natural, are threatening these trees. The combined effects of acid rain and the wooly aphid have left extensive stands of dying Fraser firs. The bone-white, leafless trunks and limbs are blatant reminders that environmental conditions are poor in the higher elevations.

The grass and heath balds along the Parkway are entirely devoid of trees. In areas like Craggy Gardens, there are entire mountainsides blanketed in rhododendron and mountain laurel. In May and June, a day of cycling along the Parkway is a study in pinks, from pale to bold.

While we are on the subject of flowers, we would like to tell you when the most notable flowers bloom in the Blue Ridge, so you can be on the lookout.

- ◆ Dogwood trees bloom from mid- to late April.
- ◆ Spring wildflowers bloom from late March to mid-May.
- ◆ Flame azalea bloom a fantastic orange in May.
- ◆ Mountain laurel bloom from late May through June.

View of the Parkway at Humback Gap Overlook (MP 6).

Skilled artisans from Europe crafted the elegant stone bridges and tunnels.

- ◆ Purple rhododendron begin blooming in mid-June.
- ◆ White rhododendron bloom in June and July.

This schedule applies to the Skyline Drive as well. An excellent, detailed "Bloom Calendar" of wildflowers along the Parkway can be found in David Catlin's book, *A Naturalist's Blue Ridge Parkway*. Catlin outlines peak bloom times and mileposts where specific flowers are most likely to be seen.

Much of the Parkway passes through wilderness areas, but scenes of rolling pasture and farmland also border the Parkway for mile upon mile. Roanoke Valley, much of Rocky Knob, Mabry Mill, Doughton Park, Boone, and Blowing Rock consist of farmland. Cabbage and corn are the primary crops grown in these areas. Much of the open hillsides are used for grazing cattle.

Apple trees are common along the Parkway; there is one major orchard right alongside the Parkway between Linville Falls and Little Switzerland. Grapes are also grown in the Blue Ridge. The vineyards of Chateau Morrisette are visible along the mountainside between Rocky Knob and Mabry Mill.

With the Parkway's often narrow boundaries and its proximity to populated areas, you must be very attentive to spot wildlife. Whereas white-tailed deer are commonplace along the Skyline Drive, it is unusual to spot them along the Parkway. Deer are very skittish and bound off as soon as you approach them. That's one advantage of traveling by bicycle. You are quiet enough to get within close range of wildlife. Woodchuck and other small mammals often forage alongside the road. Once, we set out on a dusk ride, intent upon spotting deer, and nearly wrecked trying to avoid a skunk that had wandered out onto the road. Time spent hiking or camping will reveal cottontail rabbits, raccoon, opossum, and squirrels.

The bird that has fascinated us most along the Parkway is the hawk. Broad-winged and red-tailed hawks are the most common in the Blue Ridge. Often a quick break at an overlook becomes much more when hawks are sighted soaring on the thermal updrafts that carry them for miles.

With all this said about the flora and fauna along the Parkway, there is one thing to remember. Elevation is the single overriding factor in bicycling the Parkway. It affects change in natural habitat, terrain, and weather. Elevation influences the road grades of the Parkway, determines the type of forest you cycle past, and is a factor in the weather you encounter. There are journeys within journeys along the Parkway. One day you roll alongside pastures in the 1,000- to 2,000-foot range; another day yields the challenge of 5,000- to 6,000-foot mountains.

While the Parkway does a great job of indicating major intersections and points of interest, it prohibits businesses from advertising directly on the Parkway. While some stores and hotels are easily visible from the Parkway, others are not. Be aware that roadways are marked by unobtrusive brown signs indicating road names and route numbers. Finding the proper roads is particularly challenging between Mileposts 136 south to Milepost 380.

ROCKFISH GAP TO JAMES RIVER VISITOR CENTER [0.0–64.0]

In the 115 miles from Rockfish Gap to Roanoke, the Blue Ridge narrows to a single ridge top, which the Parkway traverses, alternating from side to side. This 64-mile stretch leading to the James River Visitor Center begins with some stunning mountain overlooks. From Humpback Rocks Visitor Center, the Parkway winds upward to the rocky vantage point of Raven's Roost. If you are traveling north, this is one of your first views of the Shenandoah Valley. The rock in this area, Catoctin greenstone, has a green tint and is part of the lava flows along the Skyline Drive. When we last stood on these rocks, the view was of the sun breaking through swift-moving clouds and mist slinking along the flint-gray ridges.

This section is memorable by bicycle for its wide, arcing switchbacks, which are visible for miles ahead. The countryside varies from rocky cliffs to forests of hickory and chestnut oak and eastern hemlock to the pastures near the Whetstone Ridge wayside.

VA 664 intersects the Parkway at Milepost 13.7. This road is very steep in both directions. There is one fine facility worth visiting, a private resort called Wintergreen. Although expensive, Wintergreen is open to the public and includes lodging, food, shops, horseback riding, swimming, tennis, and golf.

The road to Sherando Lake is up ahead at Milepost 16.5. Sherando is a beautiful state park, but you have to descend down the mountain to get there. It is 5.2 miles to the park entrance and 2 miles farther to the campground.

All told, the elevation varies quite a bit in this stretch. You reach the highest point north of the James River at 3,334 feet and descend to the James River at 649 feet, the lowest elevation on the Parkway. This adds up to 4,802 feet climbed from Milepost 0 to Milepost 63. For those traveling north, the climb from the James River brings the total up to 5,990 feet.

If you are planning to make this stretch in one day, Whetstone Ridge may be a welcome breakpoint for travelers in either direction. You will cross the James River just a few miles south of Otter

Creek Campground. The James River Visitor Center features a museum and a self-guided walking trail through the river locks system that was designed to accommodate horse-pulled barges through the Blue Ridge. The original plan, developed by George Washington, was to connect waterways that extended into Ohio. Ultimately, railways replaced the barges for transporting goods.

Milepost

0.0   Rockfish Gap – US 250/I-65 (elevation 1,909 feet)

5.8   Humpback Rocks Visitor Center (elevation 2,360 feet)
You may want to tour the working farm here. The facilities include water and rest rooms. There is a ranger on duty.

8.5   Humpback Picnic Area
Tables and water

10.7   Raven's Roost (elevation 3,200 feet)
Take time to perch on these rocks and view the Shenandoah Valley.

13.7   Reeds Gap – VA 664 (elevation 2,637)
Cabin Creekwood   (540) 943-8552; www.cabincreekwood.com $$–$$$
Pleasant cabins located on the west side of Parkway. Steep 1.8 miles descent, but closer than Sherando.
Wintergreen   (804) 325-2200; www.wintergreenresort.com $$$
Wintergreen is open year-round. Proceed one mile east on VA 664. Facilities include lodging, food, gift shops, and recreational facilities.

16.0   VA 814
Royal Oak Country Store and Cabins   (800) 410-0627, (540) 943-7625; www.vacabins.com $$$
Located 0.3 miles west off Parkway, the store has some food supplies and small deli.

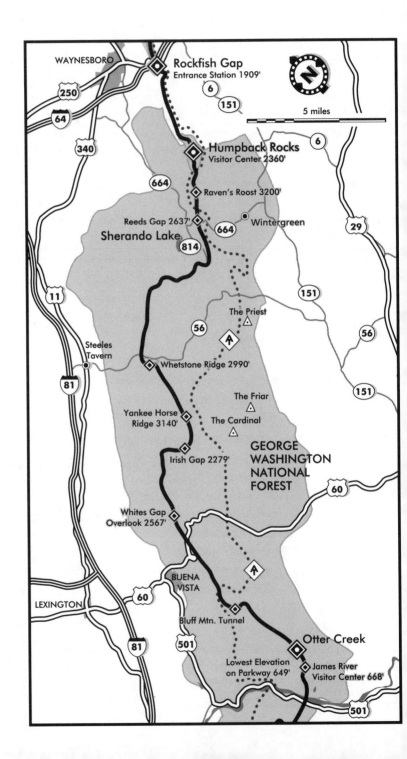

WAYNESBORO

Rockfish Gap
Entrance Station 1909'

250

151

6

64

5 miles

340

Humpback Rocks
Visitor Center 2360'

6

664

Raven's Roost 3200'

Reeds Gap 2637'

664

Wintergreen

29

Sherando Lake

814

11

151

The Priest

56

56

Steeles
Tavern

Whetstone Ridge 2990'

81

The Friar

151

Yankee Horse
Ridge 3140'

The Cardinal

Irish Gap 2279'

GEORGE
WASHINGTON
NATIONAL
FOREST

60

Whites Gap
Overlook 2567'

BUENA
VISTA

LEXINGTON

60

Bluff Mtn. Tunnel

81

501

Otter Creek

Lowest Elevation
on Parkway 649'

James River
Visitor Center 668'

501

Sherando Lake   (540) 942-5965
This national forest campground is beautiful, but it is a significant detour off the Parkway proper on VA 814, involving a total of 7.2 miles one-way. Entrance into the park is $1 for bicyclists. The camping fee is $15–$20 per campsite (open April–October). You will find free hot showers at the bathhouse. A small camp store with limited hours sells basic food items.

27.2   VA 56 (elevation 2,969 feet)
Although this highway is winding, narrow, and steep in either direction, there are two campgrounds, one east and one west of the Parkway.

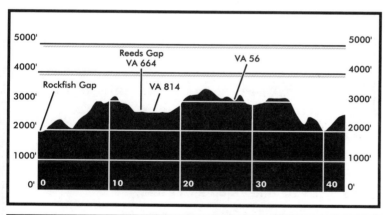

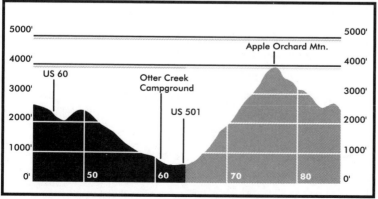

Tye River Gap Recreation Area (540) 377-6168; www.tyerivergap.com

The campground is located a very steep 1.4 miles west of intersection. There is a gravel road upon entering the campground, which has a store and laundry facilities. Open March–November, this cyclist-friendly campground offers reduced rates ($10 for individual cyclists) and indoor shelter during lousy weather.

Montebello Resort (540) 377-2650; www.montebellova.com $–$$$ (cabins)

The campground ($18 per night) and adjacent store are a very steep three miles east of Parkway. The store has snacks and limited groceries. Cabins are also available. Open April–October.

Steeles Tavern Manor (800) 743-8666, (540) 377-6444; www.steelestavernmanor.com $$$

Ready for some pampering? It is worth the trek 5.5 miles west of the Parkway in the town of Steeles Tavern, to stay at this B&B that offers luxury accommodations and fine dining. There's also an extensive video library and a VCR in each room.

29.0 Whetstone Ridge (elevation 2,990 feet)

This picnic area has water and rest rooms. Open May–October.

45.6 US 60 (elevation 2,312 feet)

Lexington Bike Shop (540) 463-7969

Need the services of a bike mechanic? It's about 11 miles (3 of them steep) west to the charming town of Lexington and the shop at 130 South Main Street. Hours: Monday–Friday, 9 a.m.–5 p.m.; Saturday, 9 a.m.–noon.

53.1 Bluff Mountain Tunnel (630 feet)

This is the first of many tunnels on the Parkway heading south. It is the only one on the Parkway in Virginia.

60.8 Otter Creek Campground & Restaurant (elevation 777 feet)

Otter Creek makes this one of the most pleasant campgrounds on the Parkway. Facilities include a restaurant and gift shop, but no camp store. Take note that there is a grocery store four miles farther south on VA 501. The campground has 45 tent sites, 24 trailer sites, and is open May–October.

63.6 James River Visitor Center (elevation 668 feet)

Make sure that you take the time out for the exhibits and the self-guided nature trail to the river locks. For information, call (804) 299-5496.

63.9 US 501

H & H Food Market & Restaurant (434) 299-5153
Follow rolling hills one mile east toward Big Island to reach this well-stocked grocery store and adjacent restaurant.

View of the James River, the lowest elevation on the Parkway.

JAMES RIVER VISITOR CENTER TO ROANOKE MOUNTAIN [64–121]

Since you are starting out at the lowest point on the Parkway and heading toward the highest point on the Parkway in Virginia, expect to do some climbing. Uphill climbs will amount to right at 4,000 feet. That's quite a bit for a mere 25 miles.

Midway into your ascent, you will encounter Thunder Ridge at 3,845 feet. This is a thickly forested area of northern red oak and Carolina hemlock. From here you will cycle past stands of striped and mountain maple at the overlook of Arnold's Valley. The Appalachian Trail parallels the Parkway throughout this section and crosses it once at Milepost 74.9.

Certainly one reason for the popularity of Peaks of Otter, named for the headwaters of the Otter River, is its proximity to numerous hiking trails. It is also one of the most extensive facilities on the Parkway with a large campground and a modest camp store. The camp store serves sandwiches and stocks basic canned goods, ice cream, and beverages. (Expect a fair amount of traffic in this area.) The lodge and restaurant have a simple mountain elegance from the gray-stained exterior to the high ceilings and exposed beams of the dining room. Views of Sharp Top and Flat Top Mountains provide the crowning touch, and Peaks of Otter, which originate from the twin peaks.

It is 35 miles from Peaks of Otter to Roanoke Mountain. The city of Roanoke sits in a valley, so the majority of this section is downhill. With both an airport and bus service, this is a possible beginning or ending point for a tour of the Blue Ridge. If you are on an extended tour, it is also the place to seek assistance for any major difficulties. The population of the Roanoke metropolitan area is over 200,000, which makes it the largest city directly off of the Parkway, though Asheville, North Carolina, runs a close second.

There are numerous access roads from the Parkway into the Roanoke area. We have investigated each side road in order to recommend the best ways to safely travel by bike into the city. If you plan to camp at Roanoke Mountain Campground, you may want to get off of the Parkway either north or south of the campground in order to stock up on food. For those seeking motels, there are several possibilities. We discovered an excellent bicycle route into downtown Roanoke (described below), which boasts a farmers market, museums, shops, and restaurants.

The best selection of motels directly off of the Parkway is 1.5 miles down US 220 North. Be careful, though, US 220 is a major highway with heavy truck traffic. Fortunately, you can pick up a frontage road, which is just a mile north and is a direct route to most facilities.

The most accessible bicycle shop in the Roanoke area is best reached from the Vinton/US 24 Exit (Milepost 112.2).

For anyone considering flying in or out of Roanoke, you should be forewarned that the airport is on the extreme north end of the city. We do not have a route to recommend from the airport to the Parkway. The most direct route is US 220. If you know you will be cycling from the airport to the Parkway, we suggest you write for a city map from the Roanoke Valley Convention and Visitors Bureau (see Appendix B).

Peaks of Otter includes one of the most extensive facilities on the Parkway.

The Parkway assumes a different character in the Roanoke area. In the Roanoke Valley, mountains are replaced by rolling farmland and the presence of a major city. Residential areas are visible from the Parkway. A true-blue naturalist might scoff at the Roanoke area, yet the opportunity to bicycle in the Blue Ridge at all is a compromise between people and their technology, and nature.

For an appreciation of the city, we recommend taking in the view from the overlook at Mill Mountain Park, just a mile from Roanoke Mountain Campground. There is a pleasant nature trail at Milepost 115, called Roanoke River Overlook, where native trees are identified. They include chestnut oak, eastern hemlock, black locust, sassafras, scarlet oak, and white pine. The trail culminates in an overlook of the Roanoke River.

For anyone traveling north to Peaks of Otter, the going is uphill. Since you are climbing up out of the Roanoke Valley, you will gain a total of 2,608 feet. Make sure you save some energy for the last five miles into Peaks of Otter, a tough stretch of steep road.

Milepost

76.7 Apple Orchard Mountain (elevation 3,950 feet)
Highest point along Parkway in Virginia

85.6 Peaks of Otter Lodge (elevation 2,525 feet) (800) 542-5927, (540) 586-1081; www.peaksofotter.com $$–$$$
Peaks of Otter Lodge is the only lodge on the Parkway open year-round. Facilities here include a restaurant, coffee shop, gift shop, and visitor center.

85.9 VA 43 South (elevation 2,875 feet)
Take the exit on the east side to head toward Bedford, Virginia.

Peaks of Otter Visitor Center
Small museum, gift store, rest rooms and water. Open May–October.

Peaks of Otter Campground   (540) 586-1614
The campground on the east side of the Parkway is
equipped with a camp store for grocery items, beverages,
and sandwiches. The campground has 90 tent sites and
53 trailer sites.

**Otter's Den Bed & Breakfast   (540) 586-2204;
www.ottersden.net $$$**
Proceed 2.2 miles on VA 43 South; a very steep descent
off the Parkway. Good views of valley from rooms.

**91.0   Bear Wallow Gap VA 695/VA 43 (elevation
2,258 feet)**
The ride to the town of Buchanan is a very steep, 4-mile
descent. Not recommended.

97.7   Black Horse Gap (elevation 2,402 feet)

105.8   US 460
A large, chain grocery store is located 1 mile west on this
very busy highway.

112.2   US 24

Vinton, Virginia
Vinton is a good place to stock up on groceries, especial-
ly if you are planning to camp at Roanoke Mountain.
Take US 24 West 0.8 mile toward Roanoke to the East
Vinton Plaza. US 24 is a four-lane highway with a small
shoulder. The East Vinton Plaza has a grocery store,
bank, and laundry.

Cardinal Bicycle   (540) 344-2453; www.cardinalbicycle.com
From the Vinton exit, follow US 24 West for 1.8 miles. US
24 will turn left, but you should continue straight on
Washington Avenue. (It becomes Gus Nicks Boulevard.)
At 3.6 miles turn right onto Orange Avenue and proceed
0.5 miles to Cardinal Bicycle on the right. Hours:
Tuesday–Friday, 10 a.m.–7 p.m.; Saturday, 9 a.m.–5 p.m.

Days Inn   (540) 342-4551 $$
Turn left onto Orange Avenue and go 1.4 miles. Located
on left. This road is a major artery and has heavy traffic.

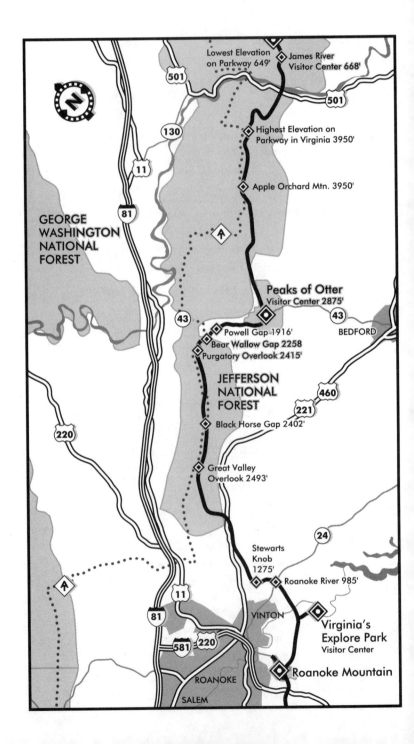

112.9 Roanoke River Overlook (elevation 985 feet)

It's a 20-minute walk on the Roanoke River Trail to an overlook of the river.

115.0 Explore Park (800) 842-9163, (540) 427-1800; www.explorepark.org

Located an easy, rolling 1.5 miles off the Parkway, the park features authentic and reconstructed buildings demonstrating Native American traditions, colonial frontier culture, and nineteenth-century life. Five miles of mountain bike trails, hiking, fishing, picnicking, a gift shop, and a tavern serving lunch and dinner round out 1,100-acre Explore Park. Admission required. Open April–October, Wednesday–Sunday.

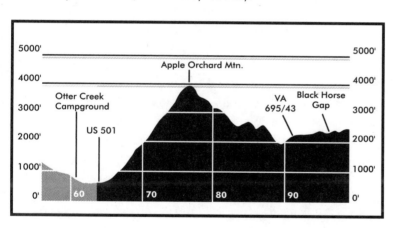

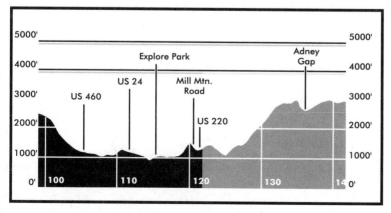

120.4 Mill Mountain Road

Mill Mountain Road takes you to Roanoke Mountain Campground, Mill Mountain Park, Roanoke Memorial Hospital, and downtown Roanoke. Because cycling in a large city is safest when you're in the know, we were determined to find the best route into Roanoke.

Ultimately, the road becomes a marked bicycle route as it parallels the Roanoke River. There is one thing we want to caution you about: This route is all downhill going into the city and all uphill going back to the Parkway. Now is the time to have an enlightened attitude about climbing hills.

What follows are our best directions into Roanoke. Turn onto Mill Mountain Road at Milepost 120.5 on the Parkway. Follow Mill Mountain Road up, around, and down the mountain. First you will pass Roanoke Mountain Campground on the left at 1.2 miles; Mill Mountain Park is 1.2 miles beyond the campground at 2.4 miles. Then you will descend down the mountain into Roanoke. Mill Mountain Road becomes Walnut Street. At 4.4 miles turn left onto Belleview Avenue. Belleview cuts through the middle of the Roanoke Memorial Hospital complex at 5 miles, and soon you will see bike-route signs. Belleview bears right onto Wiley Drive. Wiley Drive meanders alongside the Roanoke River and passes through Smith Park and passes twice over the Roanoke River. At the second bridge take the next left over the railroad crossing onto Winoa Street. The next street is Main Street. Turn left.

Roanoke Mountain Campground   (540) 982-9242
Roanoke Mountain Campground is 1.2 miles off of the Parkway on Mill Mountain Road. The only facilities here are rest rooms. There is a ranger on duty. The campground has 74 tent sites and 31 trailer sites.

Mill Mountain Zoo (elevation 1,747 feet)   www.mmzoo.org
Mill Mountain Park is located 2.4 miles from the Parkway. It features a zoological park, a wildflower garden, and an

overlook with an outstanding view of Roanoke and the Roanoke Valley. The park has a snack bar and rest rooms. Operating hours are 10 a.m.–4:30 p.m. year-round except December 25.

121.2 US 220 South

Apple Valley Motel   (540) 989-0675 $

Located 0.3 miles east of Parkway on US 220 (5063 Franklin Road).

121.4 US 220 North

US 220 North is a major highway with heavy truck traffic. Proceed with caution. It is 1.4 miles to a frontage road that will take you to numerous motels and restaurants.

Colony House Motor Lodge   (540) 345-0411 $$

Located 1.5 miles west from the Parkway on US 220 (3560 Franklin Road).

East Coasters Cycling and Fitness   (540) 774-7933; www.eastcoasters.com

East Coasters is located about 2 miles from the Parkway in the Old Country Plaza near Tangle Wood Mall. Call for directions. Open Monday–Friday, 11 a.m.–7 p.m.; Saturday, 10 a.m.–5 p.m.

The terrain undergoes a subtle metamorphosis from farmland to mountain.

ROANOKE MOUNTAIN
TO MABRY MILL [121–176]

One of the best things about the climb south, out of Roanoke, is that you have plenty of time to appreciate the views of Roanoke Valley. Between Mileposts 128 and 133, the Parkway climbs 1,800 feet with a 6.8 percent grade. Your breakfast will be long gone by the time you reach Smart View at Milepost 154.5. You can tell little about road grades along this stretch from studying the Parkway map. It is not safe to assume that since Rocky Knob is at 3,572 feet and Roanoke is at 1,425 feet you will have smooth sailing traveling north into Roanoke. Although the map leads you to expect a drop in elevation of 2,147 feet, the Parkway actually rises and descends numerous times. Likewise, these climbs make for welcome descents.

Overall, there are two major climbs for southbounders between Roanoke and Rocky Knob. The first major climb begins about six miles out of Roanoke. The second major climb begins around Rakes Millpond at Milepost 162.4 and ends beyond the Rocky Knob Campground at about Milepost 169.

There is one area on this stretch convenient for food and shelter: VA 8 at Tuggle Gap. There you will find good places to stock up on supplies or have breakfast or lunch.

We want to stress the beauty of the Rocky Knob area. Its grassy knobs are similar to those of Scotland. The huge, protruding boulders and rocks are a farmer's nightmare, but the pastoral setting of Rocky Knob is a great place to set up an easel and canvas, or to simply stand and feel the energy of the wind.

The nine miles between Rocky Knob and Mabry Mill moves through the high knobs of the Rocky Knob area, then swings down to Mabry Mill in one memorable swoop. If you are traveling south and camping at Rocky Knob, we suggest you break camp early, and cycle the vigorous nine miles to Mabry Mill for buckwheat pancakes. Arrive at Mabry Mill early to avoid standing in line.

If you are traveling north, the climbs into Rocky Knob are rewarding. The most memorable climb of this section reveals itself as a wide, rising arc in full view of the climber.

The big surprise of this section is Chateau Morrisette. Who would be expecting a winery in these parts? Less than a mile off of the Parkway at Milepost 171, this is the only winery that we know that is in such close proximity to the Parkway. Take some time out for a tour of the winery and, by all means, the wine tasting.

Mabry Mill is a certified "scenic" spot on the Parkway. Reported to be the most photographed sight on the Parkway, it is nearly always crowded. Beware of traffic when approaching the area. Mabry Mill is popular for good reason—a tour of the mill is fascinating. They still grind and sell cornmeal and buckwheat flour. Also on exhibit are a moonshine still, a sorghum mill, and a soap-making kettle. On a summer day, you may even chance upon a musician or two playing the hammered dulcimer, banjo, or mandolin.

Having the right tool for the right emergency is not always possible. Charlie performs some preventive maintenance.

Milepost

135.9 Adney Gap (elevation 2,690 feet)

150.9 VA 881/VA 640

Floyd-Franklin Turnpike is to the west and Five Mile
Mountain Road is to the east

154.1 Smart View (elevation 2,564 feet)

Smart View is a lovely picnic area with lots of shade for a
hot summer day. Rest rooms and water are available
here. The 2.5-mile Smart View trail is here.

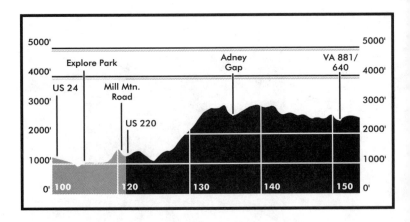

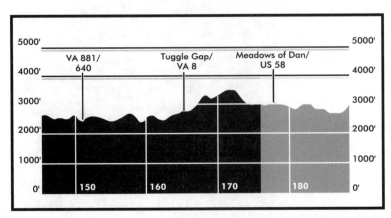

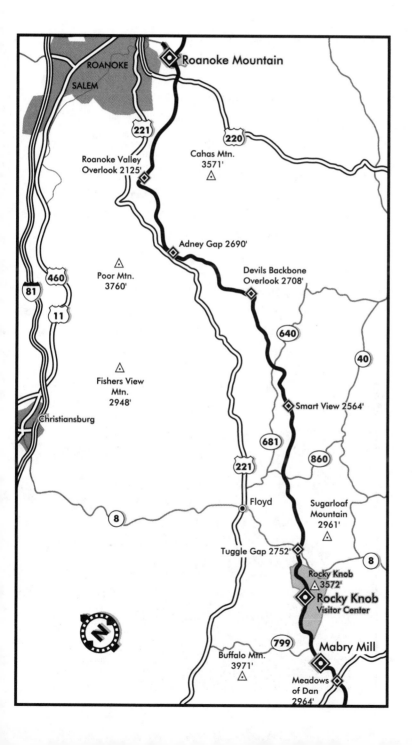

159.5 Stonewall Bed & Breakfast (540) 745-2861; www.swva.net/stonewall $$–$$$

Quaint place to rest your head located just off of the parkway. Large country breakfast provided to guests. Special spaghetti dinners for cyclists upon request. Turn onto VA 680 (Shooting Creek Road) on east side of Parkway, then make immediate left onto Wendi Pate Trail.

165.3 Tuggle Gap VA 8 (elevation 2,752 feet)

Tuggle Gap Restaurant & Motel (540) 745-3402 $

Exit onto VA 8 and turn left. Proceed 150 yards. This place doesn't look like much; the motel is very small, but the restaurant serves good food.

167.1 Rocky Knob Campground (elevation 3,572 feet) (828) 298-0398

Rocky Knob is among our favorite Parkway campgrounds. You will find an excellent trail system here. A short but steep walk to the top of Rocky Knob affords an excellent view. (Watch out for cow patties.) The campground has 81 tent sites and 28 trailer sites. Access to the 10.8-mile Rock Castle Gorge trail.

A unique display of antique farming equipment may be found at Mabry Mill.

169.0 Rocky Knob Visitor Center

Information Center, picnic area, rest rooms, phone, and access top 3.1-mile Black Ridge Trail.

171.0 Chateau Morrisette Winery (276) 593-2865; www.chateaumorrisette.com

Just past Milepost 171 look for VA 726 where you will turn right if traveling south. Make an immediate left onto VA 777 (Winery Road). The winery is less than a quarter-mile from here. The winery is open for tours Monday–Thursday, 10 a.m.–5 p.m.; Friday–Saturday, 10 a.m.–6 p.m.; and Sunday, 11 a.m.–5 p.m. Lunch and dinner are served.

171.7 Harmony Farms Bed and Breakfast (276) 593-2185; www.harmony-farm.com $$$

Turn onto VA 726 (Black Ridge Road) on west side of Parkway and go an easy 0.6 miles. Gravel road leads to house.

174.1 Rocky Knob Cabins (276) 593-3503; www.blueridgeresort.com $$

These cabins are 1 mile off the Parkway at Milepost 174; reservations are necessary. They are equipped with electric kitchens, running water, linens, dishes, and utensils.

176.2 Mabry Mill (elevation 2,855 feet)

Mabry Mill is open May–October. In addition to the mill and exhibits, there is a gift shop and restaurant. Rest rooms, drinking water, and a telephone are available. Restaurant hours: daily, 8:30 a.m.–7:30 p.m.

MABRY MILL TO CUMBERLAND KNOB [176–217]

The town of Meadows of Dan is just one mile south of Mabry Mill. Here you will find ample facilities: groceries, a laundry, restaurants, and lodging.

Relative to other sections, this 23-mile stretch is not very demanding. There is one notable climb, a little over a mile long, as you approach Groundhog Mountain, which rises to an elevation of 3,030 feet. You might want to take a break here, climb to the top of the observation tower, and study the various types of fences on display: snake rail, buck rail, and post and rail.

From Groundhog Mountain, the road rolls out toward Fancy Gap with no big surprises. The Parkway drops slightly, and you will find a straightaway of considerable length through the Orchard Gap area. Orchard Gap Deli is visible to the left.

We have two great sensory impressions of this area. One is the pungent aroma from the many fields of cabbage ready for harvest in September; the other is an abundance of flame azalea, which blooms bright orange in May.

There is a slight climb into Fancy Gap, where the elevation is 2,925 feet. Fancy Gap, visible to either side of the Parkway, is an obvious stopping place for those camping or needing a motel. For some, the distance between the Park Service campgrounds of Rocky Knob and Doughton Park will be farther than you want to push in one day. It all depends on pace, and where you are in your trip. Before you pass up the facilities at Fancy Gap, keep in mind that the distance to Doughton Park includes roughly nine miles of steady climbing.

You will cross from Virginia into North Carolina along this section. As you pedal along a shady, winding stretch of road, the Parkway makes a seamless transition from one state to the other. Upon leaving Fancy Gap, you will encounter a fairly steep climb of about a mile. There is an equal proportion of up and down all the way to Cumberland Knob.

We made up the term rolling mountain while cycling this section. When you look at the road, you just know you'll be cycling rolling hills, the kind that leave you enough momentum to crest the hill ahead of you, but this is rarely the case. Instead, you end up shifting down in the face of a climb, whether it be short or long.

This section of the Parkway is mostly pasture and farmland spread out across rolling hills. Cattle graze on small knobs with farmhouses frequently within view. Small streams trickle haphazardly alongside the Parkway. There's a timeless, down-home feel to this landscape.

Cumberland Knob was the first park constructed on the Parkway. It makes a good break point, or starting point if you are day-tripping.

One big surprise in this section is the presence of an American Youth Hostel. There is no other hostel along the Skyline Drive or the Parkway. Unless you are a member of AYH, you probably

Mayberry Trading Post (MP 180.5).

would not know this is here. It is secluded on a wonderful piece of property just off of the Parkway. The house is charming, with all the comforts of home, including a great deck in the back.

Milepost

177.7 Meadows of Dan, US 58 (elevation 2,964 feet)

Meadows of Dan is visible to either side of the Parkway. The motel and campground are just west of the Parkway, the grocery and restaurant are just east on US 58.

Meadows of Dan Food Market

This full-service grocery is open year-round.

Poor Farmers Market

This is typical of a "country store." You'll find mostly trinkets and souvenirs, but also food associated with the country-fresh produce, ham, and locally ground grits and flour.

Mountain Restaurant House

Typical Southern-style fare, offering breakfast, lunch and dinner. Open year-round.

Blue Ridge Motel & Restaurant (276) 952-2244 $

This motel and restaurant is located 75 yards west on US 58.

Meadows of Dan Campground (276) 952-2292

Open year-round with easy access from the Parkway; go west on US 58 about a half mile. Tent sites are $15; log cabins are also available.

179.4 Round Mountain Viaduct

180.5 Mayberry Trading Post (540) 952-2155

On your left traveling south, this general store is well-stocked with groceries and baked goods. On occasion, we have enjoyed traditional bluegrass music here.

188.8 Groundhog Mountain (elevation 3,025 feet)

Groundhog Mountain has an observation tower and features a display of the various types of fences constructed along the Parkway. You will find a picnic area, rest rooms, and drinking water.

**189.0 Doe Run Lodge and Restaurant
(elevation 2,950 feet) (800) 325-6189,
(276) 398-2212; www.doerunlodge.com $$$**
Just visible on the Parkway's east side, Doe Run features suites and villas with daily and weekly rates. Facilities include: tennis courts, pool, and restaurant.

189.9 Puckett Cabin Parking Area

193.5 Orchard Gap – VA 608 (elevation 2,672 feet)
**Volunteer Gap Inn and Cabins (276) 398-3689;
www.volunteergap.com $$$**
Visible from Parkway. Take gravel road west toward large sign. Luxury rooms and cabins; open year-round.

**193.7 Orchard Gap Market (elevation 2,675 feet)
(276) 398-4200; www.orchardgap.com**
This deli has sandwiches and a good selection of groceries. Open year-round. Hours: Monday–Saturday, 7 a.m.–7 p.m.; Sunday, 8 a.m.–6 p.m.

**194.7 The Inn and Cottages at Orchard Gap
(276) 398-3206;
www.bbonline.com/va/orchardgap $$$**
Look for Thunder Ridge Road on west side, go about 0.2 miles, turn left on Lightning Ridge Road.

199.4 Fancy Gap – US 52 (elevation 2,925 feet)
Fancy Gap is visible to either side of the Parkway. Motels, restaurants, a campground, and a post office are all here.
Mountain Top Restaurant & Motel (276) 728-9414 $
The restaurant is just east of the Parkway on US 52; the motel is on the west side. Open year-round.
Lake View Motel & Restaurant (276) 728-7841 $
Located west on US 52. Open year-round.
Fox Trail Campground (276) 728-7776
Go 0.2 miles west on VA 683. You will see signs for

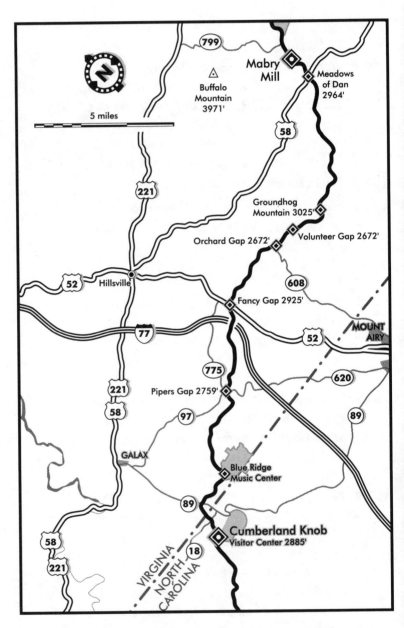

camping. This excellent campground is open year-round. Facilities include: showers, laundry, camp store, ice, and telephone.

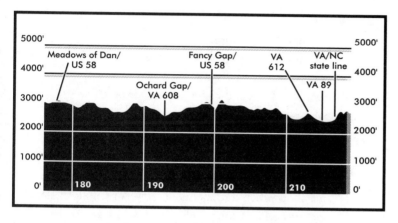

202.8 Granite Quarry Overlook (elevation 3,015)

Good views south of Pilot Mountain State Park and Hanging Rock

206.5 Felts Brothers Grocery (276) 236-6521

Just a half mile off of the Parkway; heading south on the Parkway turn right onto VA 608, left to VA 97 North. Hours: Monday–Friday, 6 a.m.–8 p.m.; Saturday, 8 a.m.– 6 p.m. It's about a half-mile moderate climb back to the Parkway.

213.3 VA 612

Blue Ridge Music Center **www.blueridgemusiccenter.com.** Supported by the National Council for the Traditional Arts, this venue offers performances by local and nationally known bluegrass and country musicians. Open to the public for performances only. Call (301) 565-0654 for more information.

214.5 Blue Ridge Country American Youth Hostel (276) 236-4962 $

This is truly a lovely place, and you don't have to be a member to stay here. You do need to bring your own food. The entrance, located on the east side, is not marked until you travel about 0.1 miles along the road. Separate dorms for men and women. Open to individuals April–October and groups (by arrangement) year-round.

215.8 VA 89

Bits and Pieces Grocery

Open year-round, this store offers snacks and drinks. If you need more substantial supplies, ride west 5 miles into Galax to Lowe's, a chain grocery store.

216.9 Virginia–North Carolina state line

217.5 Cumberland Knob (elevation 2,885 feet)

There is no camping or food here. You will find rest rooms, drinking water, and a picnic area. There is a small gift shop where a ranger is on duty. A brief trail system features a hike along Gully Creek with views of the Piedmont.

CUMBERLAND KNOB
TO NORTHWEST TRADING POST [217-259]

From Cumberland Knob southward you will encounter rolling hills with panoramic views of the Piedmont to the east. Pastureland, meadows, and apple orchards comprise much of the scenery between Milepost 217 and 230. Milepost 221.5 to Milepost 230.1 is relatively flat. This is one of the rare straight-aways on the Parkway where cycling is a breeze—enjoy. Big Pine Creek meanders from one side of the Parkway to the other.

Little Glade Pond (Milepost 230.1) marks a change in terrain. This is a pleasant break point before heading out for the climb into Doughton Park. Conversely, it makes a great place to regroup after tearing down out of the mountains from Doughton Park.

From Little Glade Pond (elevation 2,709 feet), the Parkway begins a steady 1,000-foot climb, which crests at Air Bellows Gap (elevation 3,729 feet). The terrain undergoes a subtle metamorphosis from farmland to mountain as you approach the Doughton Park area. Instead of grassy meadows, you begin to cycle past sheer rock face. Doughton Park is one of the larger parks in land area. Although you're only in the 3,000- to 4,000-foot range, south of the lodge the road will thrill you as it cuts right through mountain; you shoot past a high rock wall where the mountain was blasted to make way for the road.

Beware of gaps throughout this entire area, where gusting winds may be encountered. Cycling through gaps at high speeds can be tricky.

Signs announce Doughton Park well before facilities are encountered. Heading south, Brinegar Cabin (Milepost 238.5) is the first point of interest. The campground is next at Milepost 239.2. Deer sightings are a daily occurrence at Doughton Park, especially at dawn and dusk; try the meadow north of the campground.

If you stay overnight at Doughton Park, a climb to Bluff Mountain Overlook on the trail system should give you a fine appreciation of the feat you are accomplishing by cycling the Parkway. South from the rocky ledge of Bluff Mountain, the highway winds uphill through decidedly mountainous terrain. In fact, cycling from either direction into Doughton Park is a challenge.

Past the lodge and restaurant at Doughton Park, there are several miles of spectacular mountain scenery and cycling territory. One of the big thrills for us is the view you have of the path the Parkway takes before you actually cycle it. Where the Parkway cuts alongside Bluff Mountain, water trickles down gray-black rock that extends 50 feet up from the side of the road. It's fun to imagine what that same rock looks like in January after a few long, hard freezes. Through the winter months, the entire side of the mountain is covered in glimmering ice, inches thick.

Once out of the park, the road makes a rapid descent toward Laurel Springs. There are several miles of level cycling on the way to Laurel Springs. Laurel Springs is a touristy dot on the map with a few good facilities, and some not-so-good facilities. Miller's Campground is located roughly one mile before Laurel Springs.

Once past Laurel Springs, the Parkway climbs again. The terrain is basically rolling mountain with a few hills you can actually crest without shifting down.

If you enjoy checking out the local culture, Glendale Springs is the real treat of this area. The Church of the Frescoes and Glendale Springs Inn & Restaurant lend quaint charm to this community. Inside the Church of the Frescoes are life-sized paintings including *The Lord's Supper* and other religious scenes. A sunny country garden filled with zinnias, daylilies, poppies, and daisies surrounds the church. There is also an elaborate herb garden centered around two harps in town. One of these is an aeolian harp designed to be played by the wind.

The Northwest Trading Post is a co-op for North Carolina craftsmen. You must stop here, even if you do not venture into Glendale Springs. The Trading Post is crammed with quilts and other handcrafted items, such as lampshades decorated with pressed wildflowers, knitted afghans and sweaters, and wind chimes. The various homemade baked goods are delicious. There are country ham biscuits, hummingbird cake, molasses stack cake, peanut butter and oatmeal cookies, German chocolate cake, hoop cheese, dried apples, and more.

With camping, lodging, and so much to see, you might want to plan to make an early day of it here.

Milepost

218.6 Fox Hunters Paradise (elevation 2,805 feet)

This overlook has excellent views of the Piedmont.

229.7 US 21 (elevation 2,700 feet)

Sparta, North Carolina

Sparta is 7 miles north on US 21. This well-traveled road has truck traffic and no shoulder. There are a few big hills coming into Sparta. If you want a diversion or you need special services, this may be a good time to divert off the Parkway. Sparta has banks, laundry facilities, a hospital, and a hardware store.

Alleghany Inn **(336) 372-2501;**
www.planetnc.com/alleghanyinn $–$$
Through town on US 21; open year-round.

230.1 Little Glade Mill Pond (elevation 2,709 feet)

231.5 Inn of the Red Thread (336) 372-8743; www.innoftheredthread.com $$$

This charming bed-and-breakfast is 0.2 miles east off the Parkway on Vestal Road. Turn left at NC 1109. With breakfast included, the rates are very reasonable. This is a cycle-friendly place, offering to provide SAG support upon request. The proprietors also run a restaurant, a bakery, and an antique store. The restaurant serves breakfast every day, and dinner Friday and Saturday nights April–December

232.5 View of Stone Mountain

238.5 Brinegar Cabin (540) 587-0966

238.6 Doughton Park

Announces itself long before any facilities are encountered. There is an excellent 12-mile trail system here.

239.2 Doughton Park Campground   (540) 587-0966

This Park Service campground is separated from the restaurant and lodge by two steep miles. There is a hiking trail connecting the two facilities. There are 110 tent sites and 25 trailer sites in the campground.

241.1 Bluffs Lodge and Coffee Shop   (336) 372-4744 $$–$$$

Coffee shop hours: daily, 7:30 a.m.–7:30 p.m. The lodge, located on east side, is open May–October.

244.8 Doughton Park

Southern boundary of Doughton Park.

247.2 Miller's Camping   (336) 359-8156

Visible on the west side, Miller's Camping is open April–November. Facilities include showers, laundry, ice, and a camp store.

248.0 NC 18 (elevation 2,851 feet)

Laurel Springs, North Carolina

Laurel Springs is visible to the right of the Parkway, traveling south.

Station's Inn   (877) 528-7356; www.stationsinn.com $$

Open year-round, this motel also runs a restaurant and a well-stocked grocery store.

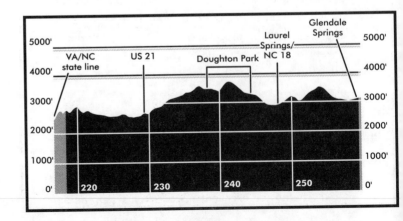

Mount Side Campground **(336) 359-2060**
Campsites and log cabins available, but it's a steep 1.3-mile climb to the campground. At press time the site was closed due to change in ownership. Call ahead of time to make sure it's operating again.

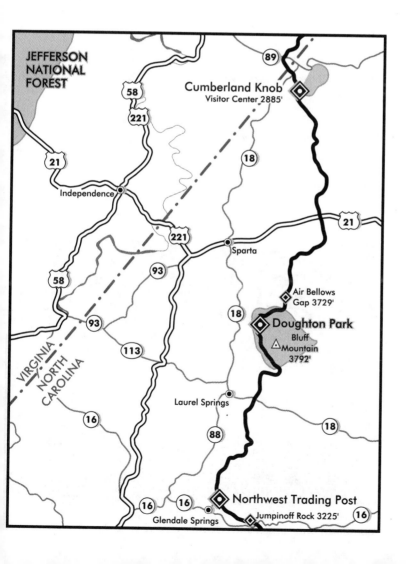

256.0 Mountain View Lodge and Cabins
(800) 903-6811; www.mtnviewlodge.com
$$–$$$

Located on the east side. Options include one- and two-bedroom cabins with kitchenettes. Breakfast is served in the lodge.

257.6 Raccoon Holler Campground   (336) 982-2706;
www.raccoonholler.com; janmill@skybest.com

Located on west side of Parkway, just north of Glendale Springs. Facilities include showers, laundry, and a camp store with grocery items.

259.0 Glendale Springs – Trading Post Road
Northwest Trading Post   (336) 982-2543

Open May 1–October 31, the Trading Post has homemade crafts and baked goods made by North Carolina craftsmen.

A sunny country garden and white picket fence surround the Church of the Frescoes.

Glendale Springs, North Carolina

There is very little indication from the Parkway of the bounty that is Glendale Springs. This is a perfect example of what can lie just yards beyond the Parkway. Turn right and head south at the Northwest Trading Post.

The Gathering Place   (336) 982-3289; www.gatheringplaceinn.com $$-$$$

Has an all-you-can-eat family-style buffet. Hours: Sunday–Thursday, 7 a.m.–8 p.m.; Friday–Saturday, 7 a.m.–9 p.m. Closed mid-December–mid-March.

Glendale Springs Inn & Restaurant   (800) 287-1200, (336) 982-2103; www.glendalespringsinn.com $$$

This historic inn is on the National Registry of Historic Places, and also has a restaurant offering fine dining. Open Thursday–Tuesday, 11 a.m.–2 p.m., 5–9 p.m.

Church of the Frescoes

In the center of town; fresco art includes "The Lord's Supper," "Mary Great With Child," and "St. John the Baptist."

NORTHWEST TRADING POST
TO LINVILLE FALLS [259–317]

There is no level ground from the trading post to Julian Price Memorial Park. You climb from the Northwest Trading Post, descend some, and then climb some more. You are headed toward Boone, Blowing Rock, and Grandfather Mountain, so higher elevations and the climbs that accompany them are inevitable.

There are several fine overlooks in this area, so at least cruise through them: view from the Lump (Milepost 264.4), Mount Jefferson Overlook (Milepost 266.9), and Elk Mountain Overlook (Milepost 274.3). At E. B. Jeffress Park there is a brief trail to Cascades Waterfall.

In the 37 miles between the Northwest Trading Post and Julian Price, the Parkway takes you through a busy area. Those traveling south are approaching a spectacular section of the Parkway. Boone and Blowing Rock are major tourist areas. Blowing Rock is far more accessible to the Parkway than Boone. It has numerous motels with a wide price range and several excellent restaurants. Boone does offer one item that Blowing Rock lacks—a bike shop—several, in fact. While Boone is a great town, it is not necessary to travel that far since Blowing Rock is nearby. However, there is a fun way into Boone via Flannery Fork Road if you are traveling on a mountain bike or have tires tough enough to withstand several miles of gravel road. See our directions that follow.

To be sure, this is a great area for mountain bikes. At Moses H. Cone Memorial Park there are over 20 miles of carriage paths that wander around the estate. Moses H. Cone is a grand estate with a stately manor house perched on a hilltop that looks down upon a man-made lake. The house and estate were donated to the Park Service. The carriage trails are used for hiking, horseback riding, and cross-country skiing. Although these trails would be ideal for mountain biking, the official policy is a firm ban on bikes. The manor house is used as a gift shop for mountain crafts and pottery. The handicrafts here are very fine and come with expensive pricetags. A vast array of pottery and hand-blown glassware, scarves and shawls made of fine wools, quilted clothing, and funky jewelry make you wish for more room in your bike bags.

At Julian Price Memorial Park you will want to be sure to get a campsite along Price Lake. If you have the time, you might want to fish for some rainbow trout or rent a canoe to go exploring. A hike around the lake after a full day of cycling would be a good way to work out the kinks. If you do camp at Julian Price, you can find food just a mile and a half south of the campground on the access road to US 221.

For the next 9 miles south of Julian Price campground, the massive, 5,837-foot broad mountain known as Grandfather Mountain is ever present, watching over the entire Boone and Blowing Rock area. Before you get to Grandfather Mountain, you will encounter an engineering masterpiece—the Linn Cove Viaduct. Cycling across the Linn Cove Viaduct is a real thrill.

The viaduct winds around Grandfather Mountain in partial suspension. The road was built away from the mountain with supports underneath. As you cycle across, you can see streams that flow underneath the viaduct and can almost reach out and touch

Slipping through a quiet length of road in Julian Price Memorial Park.

hemlock and rhododendron. Rather than whizzing past on to your next destination, you can gain a finer appreciation of the vegetation of the area and the construction of the viaduct by hiking at least part of the trail that runs parallel to the viaduct.

The viaduct is not a difficult ride. The toughest part of this section is the unrelenting five miles preceding the Linn Cove Viaduct. It doesn't look all that bad, but the grade is considerable.

Once past the viaduct, you may want to stop at the Grandfather Mountain Overlook to reflect upon what you have just passed through. If you are traveling north, the view as you approach Grandfather is spectacular.

Grandfather Mountain is an excellent side trip off of the Parkway. Privately owned, the land is protected as a natural habitat for black bear, deer, and other wildlife. At the top of the mountain, there are picnic areas, a gift shop and restaurant, and the famous suspension bridge. As you stand in the middle of the bridge, you can feel the wind's destructive power. Winds on top of Grandfather have been known to gust well past 100 miles per hour.

Pineola is the next town of note just off the Parkway, with restaurants, a motel, campground, and a post office. From Pineola, the Parkway levels out for four to five miles into a straightaway. The presence of these level stretches always amazes us, especially in the midst of such mountainous terrain.

You are now approaching the Linville Gorge Wilderness Area. You could spend weeks hiking this wild, rugged area. If you are on a mountain bike, the Forest Service roads that circle the gorge are some of the steepest we have ever cycled. From the campground at Linville Falls, it is well worth a hike to the upper and lower falls. There are views of the gorge and the surrounding Linville Mountain, Hawksbill Mountain, Table Rock, and Jonas Ridge, composed of quartzite, and you are amidst a geological history that goes back to the dinosaur days.

The Linville River attracts fly fishermen to this visitor center and campground. The river runs alongside the campsites on one side of the campground.

Milepost

268.0 Benge Gap (elevation 3,330 feet)

Park Vista Motel, Country Store & Restaurant   (336) 877-2750 $–$$

Located on the west side. If southbound, you could easily shoot past Benge Gap and miss the motel.

271.9 E. B. Jeffress Park (elevation 3,570 feet)

This park is primarily a picnic area with drinking water and rest rooms. Cascades Nature Trail is a 0.6-mile hike to the falls.

276.4 Deep Gap – US 421 (elevation 3,142 feet)

It is 1 mile toward Boone to several convenience stores. US 421 is a heavily traveled two-lane road. We do not advise going into Boone this way.

286.9 US 421

Greenes Grill

Just off Parkway going north on US 421. This restaurant is open 7 a.m.–9 p.m.

291.9 US 221 and US 321

Blowing Rock, North Carolina

There are two good routes into Blowing Rock, depending upon the direction you are traveling. If you are heading south, take US 321 toward Blowing Rock and turn right onto US 321 Business. This is an easy ride into town. For those traveling north, the best way into Blowing Rock is to take the US 221 exit before Moses H. Cone Memorial Park. It is a leisurely ride back and forth from Julian Price Memorial Path by this route. There are numerous dining and lodging possibilities in Blowing Rock. There are two notable restaurants in town: Tijuana Fats is great for Mexican food while the Blowing Rock Cafe has a wide variety of excellent dishes. For more information on accommodations and dining, call the Blowing Rock Chamber of Commerce at (800) 295-7851 or go to www.blowingrock.com.

Boone, North Carolina

Boone is accessible by two routes. The first is via US 321; it is 7 miles north on this four-lane highway. Road conditions are fairly good due to the spaciousness of the road, but traffic can be aggravated during heavy tourist seasons. There is some downhill into Boone and, likewise, a fair amount of climbing back to the Parkway. The other way in is via Flannery Fork Road for which there are signs just off the Parkway at Milepost 294.6. This road takes you right into the center of Boone. There are a couple of miles of rough, gravel road, but the road is paved at least halfway. Like Blowing Rock, there are numerous dining and lodging possibilities in Blowing Rock. For detailed

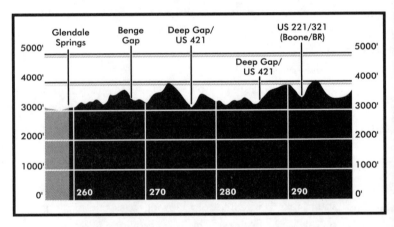

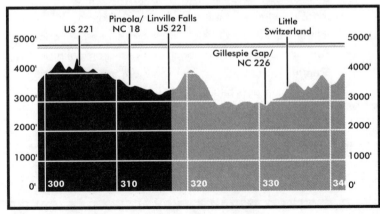

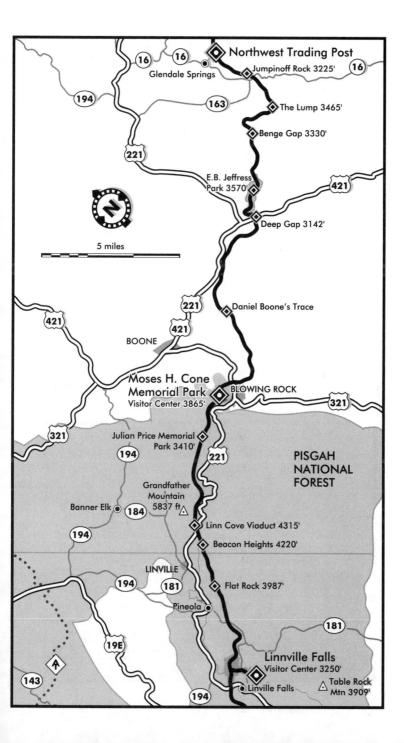

information on dining and lodging in Boone, call (800) 852-9506 or go to www.visitboonenc.com

Alpen Acres Motel   (888) 297-7881, (828) 295-7981; www.alpenacres.com $–$$

Conveniently located on the left, 0.2 miles north of Parkway on US 321.

Boone Bike & Touring   (828) 262-5750

This bike shop is located near Appalachian State University in the center of town at 899 Blowing Rock Road (US 321), across from McDonald's.

Magic Cycles   (828) 265-2211; www.magiccycles.com

Take US 321 into town, turn left on US 421, then left onto Depot Street. Located at 140 South Depot Street behind Farmers Hardware.

294.0 Moses H. Cone Memorial Park (elevation 3,865 feet)

294.6 US 221 – 2 miles into Blowing Rock

Flannery Fork Road is just off this exit.

296.4 Price Park Picnic Area

Charlie and Elizabeth perch on a balustrade in the Moses H. Cone Memorial Park.

296.9 Julian Price Memorial Park
(elevation 3,410 feet)

Price Campground

Julian Price has lakeside campsites and fishing. The campground has 129 tent sites and 62 trailer sites.

298.6 US 221/Holloway Mountain Road

Exiting left on this road will take you to US 221, which was formerly the official Parkway route before the viaduct was completed. There are a few stores less than a mile down Holloway. This is an easy trip on a bike from Julian Price Campground.

Grandfather Mountain Country (828) 295-6100

At the intersection of Holloway Mountain Road and US 221, this store has a good selection of groceries. Lunch is served here also. Open year-round, 9 a.m.–7 p.m.

304.4 Linn Cove Viaduct Information Center
(elevation 4,315 feet)

This visitor center and comfort station was built to accommodate the popularity of the Linn Cove Viaduct. The Tanawha Trail begins here. Facilities include rest rooms, telephones, and a gift shop. There is a ranger on duty.

305.1 Grandfather Mountain – US 221

Take US 221 to the right and proceed 3 miles to Grandfather Mountain. Privately owned and operated, facilities are open daily, April 1–November 15, and on winter days, weather permitting. Admission is $12 for adults, $8 for children. The road to the summit is extremely steep. For more information, call (828) 733-2013; www.grandfather.com

312 Pineola – NC 181

A spur road leads to NC 181, which leads right 1.6 miles into Pineola. There is a slight descent into town. You will find restaurants, a post office, and accommodations there.

Cyclists take cover beneath a bridge near Pineola.

Christa's Country Corner
This well-stocked grocery is open year-round and has deli. Located right off exit.

Pineola Inn & Country Store   (828) 733-4979; http://ktti.com/pineolainn $–$$
Located 1 mile from Parkway.

Down by the River Family Campground   (828) 733-5057
Mostly trailer sites with hook-ups, but there are 16 tent-only sites

316.3 Linville Falls Visitor Center
An easy, 1.5-mile road leads to parking and access to the Linville River and gorge as well as water and rest rooms. A picnic area is located just off Parkway.

Linville Falls Campground (elevation 3,250 feet)
Go 0.5 miles and look for campground on right, which has 55 tent sites and 20 trailer sites. Open year-round.

317.4 Linville Falls – US 221

Linville Falls has several motels and restaurants. The entrance to the Linville Gorge Wilderness Area is 3 miles off the Parkway, from US 221 onto NC 183, just beyond the town proper.

Parkview Motor Lodge & Restaurant   (800) 849-4452, (828) 765-4787; www.parkviewlodge.com $$

Just 0.2 miles south of the Parkway on US 221.

Linville Falls Lodge & Cottages   (800) 634-4421, (828) 765-2658; www.linvillefallslodge.com $$–$$$

This motel is 0.5 miles south of the Parkway on US 221.

Linville Falls Trailer Lodge and Campground (828) 765-2681; www.linvillefalls.com

Go 0.2 miles south on US 211, then turn right on Gurney Franklin Road and go 1 mile.

Skyline Mini-Mart

Head south 0.3 miles on US 211; it's on the right. Open April–November.

Famous Louise's Rock House restaurant

Go south on US 211 for 0.7 miles. On right.

Spear's Restaurant   (868) 765-2658

Go south on US 211 for 0.7 miles. On left across from post office. Great North Carolina barbecue!

LINVILLE FALLS TO CRAGGY GARDENS [317–364]

Linville Falls and Crabtree Meadows are both wonderful areas from which to make day trips. You could set up base camp at either place and have plenty of options for exploring by bicycle. The various motels in Little Switzerland all make wonderful weekend getaways.

One of the highlights of this area is the vast apple orchard between Mileposts 328 and 329. In the fall, you can buy quite an assortment of apples, including Stayman Winesap, Stark's Delicious, and York Imperial. If you are lucky enough to cycle through here between late April and early May, the apple blossoms will intoxicate you with their perfume.

NC 226 intersects the Parkway at Milepost 331. A side trip to Spruce Pine may not be necessary, but you can find grocery stores, restaurants, motels, and banks there. The Museum of North Carolina Minerals is located at this intersection. Time spent with the exhibits will give you an appreciation of the geology and mineralogy of the Blue Ridge. Displays of amethyst, quartz, emerald, mica, and other rocks and minerals native to the Blue Ridge explain the fascination rock hounds have with the area.

Little Switzerland is a pleasant side trip right off of the Parkway at Milepost 334. There are three excellent motels here. This is a good place to treat yourself. Beyond this point heading south, there are very few accommodations until you reach Asheville. If you like to browse in shops, there are several good ones in Little Switzerland.

Little Switzerland Tunnel begins the start of many tunnels from here to Cherokee. You may want to mount a lighting system from here on out. If nothing else, a flashing belt beacon on your rear will alert cars to your presence.

Crabtree Meadows has a campground, a restaurant, and a camp store. These are the last facilities on the Parkway proper until Mount Pisgah, which is 70 tough miles away. We recommend getting a motel room in Asheville so you can get cleaned up and fresh for the grueling climb from Asheville to Mount Pisgah.

Enjoy the fantastic descent you get in this section. From Chestoa View, elevation 4,090 feet, you will drop down to 2,819 feet at Gillespie Gap. That's almost ten miles of pure downhill. From Gillespie Gap you will begin a climb into the Black Mountains, which culminates with Mount Mitchell at 6,684 feet.

Speaking of Mount Mitchell, just how big of a deal can one mountain be? Just ask anyone who has done the annual Assault on Mount Mitchell. If you are undertaking the Parkway in a big way, you owe it to yourself to cycle to the top of Mount Mitchell. You don't want to deny yourself the opportunity of being able to say you've cycled up to the highest peak east of the Mississippi River. The gain in elevation on the 4.8-mile spur road to the summit is 1,390 feet. The view is unparalleled. The descent is nerve-tingling. The damage to the spruce and fir forests by the woolly aphid and acid rain should be witnessed. Motorists will think you are crazy, but Mount Mitchell is a bicyclist's mecca.

For those wondering what the Assault on Mount Mitchell is all about, it's a 102-mile endurance event open to anyone crazy enough to try it. Sponsored by the Spartanburg Freewheelers, the event begins in Spartanburg, South Carolina in late May. In 1998

The Assault on Mount Mitchell is an arduous event held each year.

there were 750 participants, the maximum number allowed on the Parkway by the National Park Service. For more information, contact the Freewheelers at (800) 636-6773, ext. 6664, or go to their website at www.freewheelers.info.

Camping at Mount Mitchell State Park allows you a chance to experience the harsh weather conditions characteristic of the higher elevations. These campsites are not fully exposed, but they are situated on the side of the mountain. Mist or rain is likely. The gusting winds characteristic of the mountain are sure to whip your little nylon tent all through the night. There are only nine sites here and they are fairly primitive. Don't expect asphalt leading up to your tent pad. Arrive before noon in order to get one of these precious sites.

The Parkway is spectacular from Mount Mitchell to Craggy Gardens. You are in the midst of the Black Mountains and they deliver. This entire area is a cyclist's dream. Granted, you have to work extremely hard, but that always serves to heighten the experience. We would feel cheated if we drove in a car through this area. Once you've traveled the Parkway on a bike, you won't want to do it any other way.

Craggy Gardens is known for its rhododendron. Hiking trails take you to the top of the bald where the view of the Black Mountains is supreme. In addition to rhododendron, there are mountain laurel, blueberry, mountain cranberry, and mountain ash all in abundance. Mountain ash grab your attention in the late fall, after the leaves have fallen, when their brilliant red berries provide the only bright color.

Milepost

324.8 Bear Den Family Campground
(828) 765-2888; www.bear-den.com

Be on the lookout for Bear Den Mount Road on the east side of Parkway. 0.6 mile to the campground. this road. A moderately steep, rough-paved road leads to the campground. This campground is well managed with showers, laundry, and a camp store. Tent sites open March–November.

328.1 Alta Pass

The Orchard at Alta Pass   (888) 765-9531;
www.altapassorchard.com
Located on east side, this store has souvenirs, ice cream, and light snacks. Music, hay rides, and more. Open May–October.

331.0 Gillespie Gap – NC 226 (elevation 2,814 feet)

Museum of North Carolina Minerals   (704) 765-2761
Located right off the Parkway, this Park Service museum features excellent exhibits of area rocks and minerals. A bookstore, rest rooms, and drinking water are available. NC 226 intersects here. You can take a back way into Little Switzerland via NC 226A. If you turn left and go under the bridge, you will find a motel and convenience store.

Pine Valley Motel   (828) 765-6276;
www.pinevalleymotel.com $$
About 3.5 miles from the Parkway going north on NC 226. Open year-round.

Spruce Pine, North Carolina
Spruce Pine is a whopping 6 miles from the Parkway going north on NC 226. There are two major grocery stores, a drug store, a hardware store, banks, and restaurants.

Skyline Motel & Restaurant   (828) 765-9394 $
Located east of Parkway on NC 226A.

Mountain View Motel & Restaurant   (800) 304-1715,
(828) 765-4233; www.mountainviewmotel.com $
From Parkway, take NC 226 beneath tunnel. Located on right.

333.4 Little Switzerland Tunnel (542 feet)

334.0 Little Switzerland, North Carolina – NC 226A

Maybe call it an early day and hang out for the afternoon.

Alpine Inn   (828) 765.5380;
www.insidenc.com/alpineinn.htm $–$$
This motel is the farthest from the Parkway, but it is dear to our hearts. It has the most reasonable rates, too. Turn

right onto NC 226A and travel south 1 mile; steep return to the Parkway. Open late April–early November.

Big Lynn Lodge   (828) 765-4257, (800) 654-5232; www.biglynnlodge.com $$$

Visible on east side of Parkway. A hearty dinner and breakfast are included in the price. From Parkway exit,

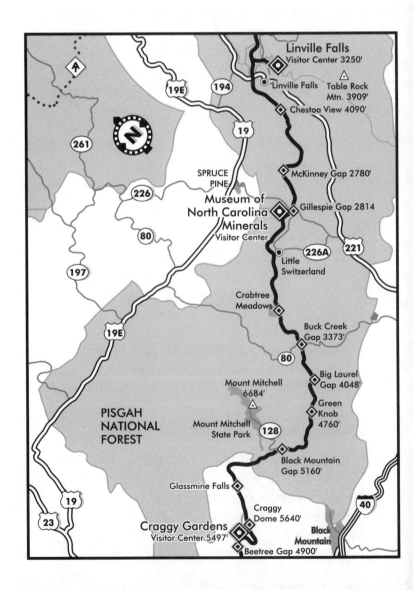

turn left on NC 266A and go about 1 mile. Open
April–October.

**Switzerland Inn   (828) 765-2153; www.switzerlandinn.com
$–$$$**
Located on left immediately off of Parkway, this elegant
lodge was established in 1910. For the economy minded,
the inn has a bunkhouse with eight rooms connected to a
central living room. Breakfast for two is included. If you
prefer a little pampering, stay at the inn proper. Wonderful
views of the valley lie below.

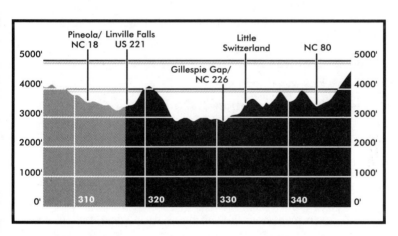

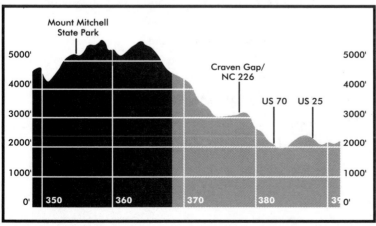

Switzerland Café and General Store (828) 765-5289; www.switzerlandcafe.com

On the way to the Alpine Inn, you can get gourmet deli sandwiches here.

336.8 Wildacres Tunnel (330 feet)

339.5 Crabtree Meadows

Crabtree Meadows has 71 tent sites and 22 trailer sites. Crabtree Falls is a 40-minute walk from the campground.

Crabtree Meadows Coffee Shop (828) 675-4236

Coffee shop and camp store stocked with basic grocery items. We just wish that the food counter opened earlier for breakfast. With a strenuous 5-mile round-trip to Mount Mitchell ahead for southbounders, breakfast is a must. Restaurant hours: daily, 9:30 a.m.–6 p.m.

340.2 Crabtree Meadows Picnic Area

Has water and rest rooms.

344.0 NC 80 (elevation 3,373 feet)

There are just a few recommended facilities within close range of this intersection.

Carolina Hemlock Recreation Area (702) 682-6146

This Pisgah National Forest campground has a bracing mountain stream that feeds a deep swimming pool, but it is 6 miles north toward Burnsville. Cycling to Carolina Hemlock from Crabtree Meadows or Little Switzerland and back makes an outstanding day trip.

Mount Mitchell View Restaurant

Located 1.5 miles north on NC 80; a very steep descent and return.

344.5 Twin Tunnel (North) (300 feet)

344.7 Twin Tunnel (South) (401 feet)

349.0 Rough Ridge Tunnel (150 feet)

355.4 Mount Mitchell State Park

The road to the summit is a 5-mile climb with grades reaching 8 percent. This is much steeper than any other grade on the Skyline Drive or the Parkway. Actually, the first two miles to the summit are steeper than the last three. There's a snack bar, natural history museum, and observation tower at the top. The campground is four miles from the Parkway. Remember, there are only nine campsites and they are first-come, first-served. There is a restaurant here also, but it sometimes closes during the peak season. Open May–October. Restaurant hours: Monday–Friday, 11 a.m.–8 p.m.; Saturday–Sunday, 8 a.m.–8 p.m.

361.2 View of Glassmine Falls

A 0.1-mile trail leads to view of this 800-foot falls.

364.1 Craggy Dome Parking Overlook (elevation 5,640 feet)

364.4 Craggy Pinnacle Tunnel (245 feet)

364.4 Craggy Gardens (elevation 5,497 feet)

Craggy Gardens has a visitor center with rest rooms, drinking water, and a good selection of literature on the Blue Ridge. Take a hike to Craggy Dome, Craggy Pinacle, and Craggy Knob.

367 Bee Tree Gap – Craggy Gardens Picnic Area

It has 86 sites, rest rooms, and is wheelchair accessible.

CRAGGY GARDENS TO MOUNT PISGAH
[364–406]

Get ready for some fun. You have a solid ten miles of spectacular downhill into Asheville. You'll gain it back if you are cycling on to Mount Pisgah, but for now, enjoy. Pisgah National Forest spreads its lush blanket of green as far as the eye can see. The Swannanoa River Valley and the town of Black Mountain are to the east.

Known as "The Land of the Sky," Asheville is the quintessential city of the Blue Ridge. With a population of 160,000, it has become an urban center in its own right. Its burgeoning size warrants some careful directions on how to get around. We suggest you take one of two routes to reach the inner city. Town Mountain Road leads to downtown Asheville and two bike shops. The route through Biltmore Forest situates you best for the Biltmore Estate. A third route is best for reaching the airport. We outline each route below.

Of modern design in wood and stone, the Folk Art Center sits serenely in its mountain setting. If you appreciate fine handicrafts, you will want several hours to spend here. Bring your credit card, because the artsy jewelry, hand-loomed fabrics, and original pottery are expensive. The Folk Art Center also has an extensive selection of books on the southern highlands.

There are numerous tourist attractions in Asheville. The Biltmore Estate, the Thomas Wolfe Memorial and home, and the seasonal festivals held in Asheville are all reasons to spend some time in the city. If you plan on touring Asheville, you may want to write the Asheville Travel and Tourism Office for detailed information (see Appendix B).

Past Asheville, over a 12-mile section between Milepost 397 and 409, you'll encounter nine tunnels, ranging in length from 275 to 1,320 feet. Pine Mountain Tunnel at Milepost 399.1 is the longest on the Parkway. Let your imagination run wild with the names of the tunnels as you travel through them: Buck Spring, Ferrin Knob, Grassy Knob, Young Pisgah Ridge, Fork Mountain . . . you'll need the diversion with all of the climbing you've got to do.

From Milepost 384 to Milepost 408, you will climb 3,705 feet. You may have to get off your bike and cry, but you'll make it. This is why Asheville is such a good break point for cyclists doing extended tours. Whether you are traveling north or south, you will have a climb out of Asheville. Take heart if you are touring the Parkway north to south. The climb from Asheville to Mount Mitchell is worse, at a grand total of 4,265 feet climbed to the entrance of Mount Mitchell State Park.

At Milepost 399.7 you might want to stop and view Pisgah Ridge rising up to the 5,749-foot peak of Mount Pisgah. You will be traveling across Pisgah Ridge because the Parkway follows it for 24 miles to Tanasee Bald. At Tanasee Bald the Parkway enters the Great Balsam Range.

The historic presence of the Vanderbilts is evident upon reaching Mount Pisgah. In the late 1800s, George Washington Vanderbilt bought 130,000 acres of land in the area, including Mount Pisgah. Remnants of a stone foundation are all that are left of Vanderbilt's mountain retreat at Buck Spring Gap.

Pisgah Inn is truly a mountain retreat. It hugs the side of the mountain, and the floor-to-ceiling picture windows in the dining room and each of the guest rooms frame views of the hazy blue ridges toward Hendersonville and Brevard. Pisgah Inn is the place to sample rainbow trout, prepared here five different ways.

Camping here is enjoyable; with an excellent store and restaurant dining as an option, you have plenty of resources at your disposal. A day or two spent here is full of possibilities. The steep hike to the magnificent Mount Pisgah can occupy an entire afternoon. There's a weather station and an observation tower at the summit. It's windy at the top, and weather changes can be sudden, so bring a jacket. Additional hikes, in all directions from the campground, make for plenty of exploring.

Mountain laurel and several varieties of rhododendron, including catawba, Carolina, and rosebay, are abundant in the campground, as well as a couple miles farther on in the Cradle of Forestry. An overlook at Milepost 410.3 reveals the Pink Beds, part of the Cradle of Forestry area of Pisgah National Forest, which are a dense undergrowth of mountain laurel and rosebay rhododendron interspersed with tiny mountain bogs. Late May through June is the time to find the rhododendron and laurel in bloom. Wildflowers are prolific all summer throughout the campground and the grounds surrounding the inn.

Milepost

365.5 Craggy Flats Tunnel (400 feet)

374.4 Tanbark Ridge Tunnel (780 feet)

377.4 Craven Gap – NC 694 (Town Mountain Road) (elevation 3,132 feet)

Exiting the Parkway here places you in downtown Asheville and near several hotels, restaurants, and bike shops. Town Mountain Road is a two-lane scenic highway that winds through a residential area. (Warning: There's no shoulder on this busy, narrow road.) From the Parkway, Town Mountain Road climbs for about 2 miles and then descends the mountain into Asheville. Be careful on the switchbacks on the steep descent into town. Turn right onto College Street, about 6.5 miles from the Parkway. At the second traffic light, turn right onto Oak Street, which turns almost immediately into Woodfin Street.

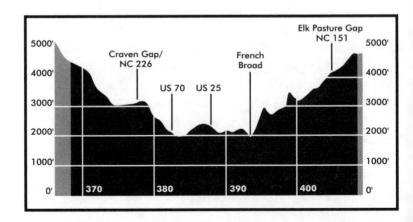

Hearn's Cycling & Fitness   (828) 253-4800

Follow Town Mountain Road route above, continuing on Woodfin Street to second light. Turn left and look for shop on left, several blocks up. Total mileage from the Parkway to Hearn's is 7.5 miles. Hours: Monday–Saturday, 8:30 a.m.–5:30 p.m.

Bio-Wheels   (828) 232-0300; www.biowheels.com

Follow Town Mountain Road route above, continuing on Woodfin Street to second light. Turn left. Continue

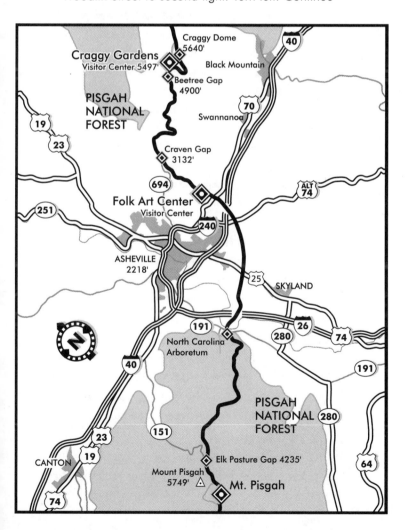

through downtown Asheville about 0.3 miles and look for shop on left. This busy road continues to the Biltmore Estate, US 25, and reentry onto Parkway.

Ski Country Sports   (828) 254-2771
Follow Town Mountain Road route above, continuing on Woodfin Street to second light. Turn right onto Broadway, which soon turns into Merrimon Avenue. Go about 4 miles north to 1000 Merrimon Avenue. Store is on left. There are a laundromat and large grocery store nearby.

Pro Bikes of Asheville   (828) 253-2800; www.pro-bikes.com
This bike shop relocated several miles beyond downtown across the French Broad River to west Asheville at 610 Haywood Road. Call for directions. Hours: Monday–Friday, 10 a.m.–7 p.m.; Saturday, 10 a.m.–5 p.m.; Sunday, closed (opens at 11 a.m. in January and February).

Best Western   (828) 253-1851 $$–$$$
Located on right at 22 Woodfin Street.

American Court   (800) 233-3582, (828) 253-4427; www.americancourt.com $$
Follow Town Mountain Road route above, continuing on Woodfin Avenue to second light. Turn right onto Broadway, which soon turns into Merrimon Avenue. Located on right at 85 Merrimon Avenue.

Renaissance Hotel Asheville   (828) 252-8211 $$$
Located on left off of Woodfin Street, across from Best Western.

382.0   Folk Art Center
Operated by the Southern Highland Handicraft Guild, this is a required stop for anyone interested in crafts, books, or history and information on the Blue Ridge. Rest rooms and drinking water are available here.

382.5   US 70 intersection
The closest facilities are just 1 mile east on US 70 toward Black Mountain. There are numerous motels and several restaurants.

Motel 6 (828) 299-3040 $

Travelodge East (828) 298-5140 $–$$

Holiday Inn East (828) 298-5611 $$–$$$

Super 8 Motel (828) 670-8800 $$–$$$

Heading west on US 70 toward Asheville, you will find a grocery store, post office, banks, and a medical facility. Asheville Medical Center is located 1.3 miles from the Parkway on US 70 West.

383.5 I-40 crosses underneath the Parkway (elevation 2,040 feet)

384.7 US 74 intersection

Avoid this interchange. There is nothing here of note.

388.1 US 25

This is our recommended exit for the Asheville Airport and the most accessible bike shop in Asheville, Liberty Bicycles. You can take US 25 into Asheville, but it is a well-traveled, two-lane highway. There are major shopping centers within a quarter mile of the Parkway in either direction on US 25.

The Folk Art Center is a required stop for anyone interested in Appalachian folk art.

Liberty Bicycles (828) 274-2453; www.libertybikes.com
Take US 25 north 0.3 miles toward Asheville. Located in
strip mall on right by major grocery store (1378
Hendersonville Road). Hours: Monday–Friday, 10 a.m.–
7 p.m.; Saturday, 10 a.m.–6 p.m.; Sunday, 1–5 p.m.

Asheville Airport
Follow US 25 South (a four-lane highway) to Airport
Road. Turn right onto Airport Road and follow to airport.
This entire area is congested.

Biltmore Estate
At the US 25 exit, we found a beautiful route into the
tourist area of Asheville. Biltmore Estate is only 4 miles
via this route. On the way, you get to cycle through one
of the most elegant neighborhoods in Asheville. Take the
US 25 South exit and turn left into Biltmore Forest. Take
an immediate right onto Stuyvesant Road. Follow this
road about 2 miles until it merges onto Vanderbilt Road.
You will bear right here. Vanderbilt Road ends at the
Biltmore Dairy Bar (115 Hendersonville Road, phone
(828) 274-1501), which features delicious ice cream. It is
3.6 miles from the Parkway to the Dairy Bar. Biltmore
Estate is a quarter mile to your left from the light. You are
in the midst of Biltmore Village, which has numerous gift
shops. There are several motels in the area.

Forest Manor Inn (828) 274-3531;
www.forestmanorinn.com $$$
Located 1.7 miles north of the Parkway on US 25; a
moderate climb to return on a four-lane highway with a
wide shoulder. 866 Hendersonville Road

Doubletree Hotel (828) 277-1800 $$$
Located at 115 Hendersonville Road in general area of
Biltmore Dairy Bar.

The Quality Inn (828) 684-6688 $$–$$$
The Quality Inn is adjacent to the Biltmore Dairy Bar at 1
Skyline Inn Drive.

Biltmore Howard Johnson Lodge (828) 274-2300 $–$$
190 Hendersonville Road. Visible from the Dairy Bar,
right on Hendersonville Road.

Plaza Motel (828) 274-2050 $–$$
11 Hendersonville Road. Left from the Dairy Bar on
Hendersonville Road.

Holiday Inn Express (828) 274-0101 $$–$$$
Located 3.2 miles north on US 25, 234 Hendersonville
Road.

393.6 French Broad River (elevation 2,000 feet)
NC 191 intersects the Parkway here. There are picnic
areas along the river just off of the Parkway in both directions. There are a few facilities on NC 191 north, but this
is a narrow, two-lane highway.

North Carolina Arboretum (828) 665-2492;
www.ncarboretum.org
Several miles of trails wind through this wonderful
resource for learning about trees and plants. Open year-
round. No parking fee for bikes.

Carolina Fatz (828) 665-7744
This bike shop is 1.5 miles north on NC 191. This is a
very busy road. Open Monday–Saturday, 10 a.m.–6 p.m.

Lake Powhatan Recreation Area (828) 670-5627
This Pisgah National Forest campground is quite a detour
from the Parkway. It's only 3 miles off of the Parkway, but
it's mostly downhill.

397.1 Grassy Knob Tunnel (770 feet)

399.1 Pine Mountain Tunnel (1,434 feet)
This is the longest tunnel on the Parkway.

400.9 Ferrin Knob Tunnel No. 1 (561 feet)

401.3 Ferrin Knob Tunnel No. 2 (421 feet)

401.5 Ferrin Knob Tunnel No. 3 (375 feet)

403.0 Young Pisgah Ridge Tunnel (412 feet)

404.0 Fork Mountain Tunnel (389 feet)

404.7 Elk Pasture Gap – NC 151 (elevation 4,235 feet)

406.9 Little Pisgah Tunnel (576 feet)

407.3 Buck Springs Tunnel (462 feet)

407.8 Mount Pisgah Picnic Area (elevation 4,900 feet)

**408.6 Pisgah Inn   (704) 235-8228;
www.pisgahinn.com $$$**

Pisgah Inn's reputation precedes it. Reservations are
strongly suggested. At the very least, treat yourself to a
meal here. You deserve it after your crazy cycling antics.
You will also find telephones and a camp store here.
Open April–October.

**408.8 Mount Pisgah Campground
(elevation 4,850 feet)   (828) 235-8228**

The campground is on the west side, near the Pisgah Inn.
The campground has 70 tent sites and 70 trailer sites.

None of the tunnels, including the 665-foot Devil's Courthouse Tunnel,
have artificial lighting.

MOUNT PISGAH TO CHEROKEE [409–469]

It is 60 rugged miles to Cherokee, and you had better be well prepared. Facilities are scarce in these parts. You will be cycling along Pisgah Ridge to the Great Balsams. You will reach the highest point on both the Skyline Drive and the Blue Ridge Parkway at Richland Balsam, elevation 6,053 feet. Stop here and take it all in. You have truly come far if you have cycled from Front Royal to this point. It is a major achievement to get here from Cherokee or Asheville.

"Awesome" describes this section of the Parkway. From Mount Pisgah, the first geologic feature to command your attention is Looking Glass Rock. Its prominent, bare granite dome has become quite famous. After five or six preliminary miles of ups and downs, the Parkway begins the long ascent to Richland Balsam. Graveyard Fields and Graveyard Ridge are eerie in their barren, flat appearance described as "bog-like" because of their lack of trees. In 1925, a forest fire destroyed 25,000 acres of spruce-fir forest. Today, the forest is slowly recovering: The "fields" are now filled with blueberries, mountain laurel, rhododendron, and bush honeysuckle.

It could be argued that the best way to appreciate this area is by foot. Many areas of these mountains are accessible only by hiking trails. The Shining Rock Wilderness Area is 13,400 acres of wild mountain terrain. A spur road at Milepost 420.2 takes you to Ivestor Gap, where the hiking trails begin. You might have time to take a brief hike to the top of Devil's Courthouse, by way of the trail at Milepost 422.4, on your way to Cherokee. When mists hug this rocky, rugged summit it looks devilish for sure.

The manner in which the trees grow in this section is something you can appreciate as you make the arduous climb to Richland Balsam. Fraser fir and red spruce are symbols of these mountains. They are the true inhabitants, able to survive the brutal climate of higher elevations. The one disturbing thing about cycling through Richland Balsam is the sight of the dead Fraser fir that cover the highest peaks. Just as with Mount Mitchell, the

125

Fraser fir is dying because of an insect called the balsam woolly aphid and other environmental stresses such as acid rain. It is hoped that ultimately the Fraser fir will be able to genetically adapt to this parasite.

Logic would follow that since you have just cycled to the highest point on the Parkway then, surely, you will now have a great descent. Well, you do. You also have a climb back up to Waterrock Knob before the final descent into Cherokee. The grand total of elevation climbed in this entire stretch is 6,225 feet. For those cycling from Cherokee to Mount Pisgah, you will have to endure a total climb of 9,305 feet. The major portion of this climb, 7,470 feet, is from Cherokee to Richland Balsam.

There has been some debate over which direction is tougher for cyclists, north to south or south to north. The general consensus is that the Parkway is tougher traveling south to north. In fact, the total feet climbed is higher in this direction, but not by much: 48,722 feet versus 48,601 feet. (See Appendix B for details.)

What options do you have if you can't cycle this section in a single day? Well, Balsam Mountain campground isn't a lot of

When you head away from Mount Pisgah, Looking Glass Rock is just to the left.

help. The spur road up to it climbs an additional 1,100 feet, and all you've got left is a ten-mile descent into Cherokee. Your single alternative for lodging and food is the exit toward Waynesville at Balsam Gap, Milepost 443.1. This is an easy descent toward the town of Balsam, where you will find food, a motel, and a campground. Aside from this, the only feasible exit we know of is at Soco Gap. Any other way off of the Parkway involves a major descent and too many miles detoured off the Parkway.

The descent into Cherokee is a cyclist's dream. Don't get carried away in the tunnels. They are much more dangerous when you are traveling at top speeds. There are six tunnels between Soco Gap and Cherokee.

Milepost

410.1 Frying Pan Tunnel (577 feet)

411.9 Wagon Road Gap – US 276
(elevation 4,535 feet)

**Cradle of Forestry in America Visitor Center
(828) 884-5713**
It is a steep 4-mile descent from the Parkway on US 276 South. If your base camp is Mount Pisgah, this would be a good side trip. The visitor center has exhibits, a movie, and interpretive trails. Open daily, 9 a.m.–5 p.m. April–November. An entrance fee of $5 is charged.

**Back Country Outdoors   (828) 884-4262;
www.backcountryoutdoors.com**
This bike shop is in the town of Pisgah Forest, 15 miles from the Parkway on US 276 South.

422.1 Devil's Courthouse Tunnel (665 feet)

423.3 Beach Gap – NC 25 (elevation 5,340 feet)

431.4 Richland Balsam Overlook
(elevation 6,053 feet)
Highest point on the Blue Ridge Parkway.

439.7 Pinnacle Ridge Tunnel (813 feet)

443.1 Balsam, North Carolina – US 23/74 (elevation 3,370 feet)

Balsam Mountain Inn **(800) 224-9498, (828) 456-9498; www.balsaminn.com** **$$$**

Elegant accommodations located 1.7 miles from the Parkway, complete with library, porches, great room, country breakfast, lunch, and dinner. Go south on US 23/74. In between highway mile markers 93 and 94, turn left on Candelstick Lane then sharp right on Cabin

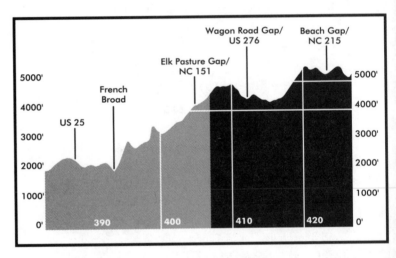

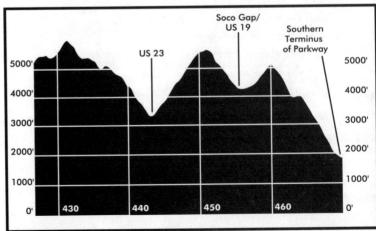

Flats Drive. Follow road across railroad tracks (twice).
Located on hill on left.

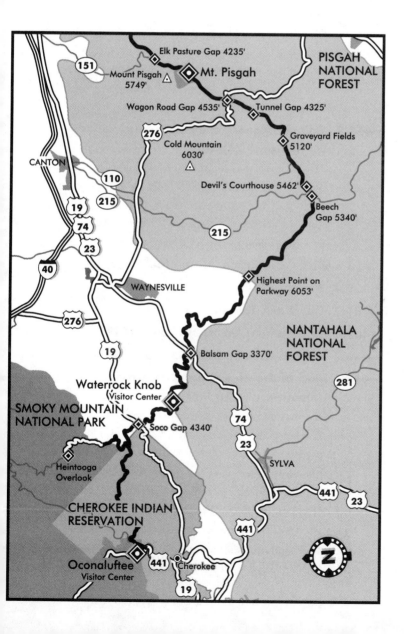

451.2 Waterrock Knob Parking Overlook
(elevation 5,718 feet)

You will find rest rooms and drinking water here.

455.7 Soco Gap – US 19
(elevation 4,340 feet)

It is 5 miles straight down to Maggie Valley on a two-lane highway.

Starvin' Marvin Service Station (704) 926-3635

This convenience store is just 0.3 mile on US 19 South. They allow tent camping here.

458.2 Balsam Mountain Campground
(elevation 5,240 feet)

The campground at Balsam Mountain is part of Great Smoky Mountains National Park. Take Heintooga Spur Road 8.6 miles to the campground with a gain in elevation of 1,100 feet. There are 40 campsites here. Facilities include drinking water and rest rooms.

458.8 Lickstone Ridge Tunnel (402 feet)
459.3 Bunches Bald Tunnel (255 feet)
461.2 Big Witch Tunnel (348 feet)
465.6 Rattlesnake Mountain Tunnel (395 feet)
466.2 Sherril Cove Tunnel (550 feet)
469.1 End of the Blue Ridge Parkway
(elevation 2,020 feet)

For the record, the Parkway is actually 470 miles long. The Linn Cove Viaduct altered the total mileage. There are no immediate plans to change the mileposts.

Cherokee, North Carolina (elevation 2,020 feet)

You are now connected with Great Smoky Mountains National Park. It is 2 miles south of Cherokee by way of US 441. There are numerous lodging possibilities.

Best Western Great Smokies Inn (828) 497-2020 $$$

Off Big Cove Road, 0.8 miles from the Parkway entrance.

Baymont Inn   (828) 497-2102 $$–$$$
Located 1 mile south of Parkway on Acquiona Road

Sleep Inn   (828) 497-4730 $$–$$$
Located about 1 mile south of Parkway on US 441 South.

Cherokee KOA   (828) 497-9711
On US 441 South take the first left to Big Cove Road and follow signs 4 miles to campground. You'll find a pool and a camp store here.

Newfound Lodge   (828) 497-2746 $$
On the Oconaluftee River located 1 mile from the Parkway entrance on US 441 North.

Riverside Motel & Campground   (828) 497-9311 $$
Located 0.75 mile south of Cherokee on US 441. Waterfront rooms and campsites.

GREAT SMOKY MOUNTAINS NATIONAL PARK

You can continue for 33 miles from Cherokee to Gatlinburg through Great Smoky Mountains National Park on US 441. The road is similar in character to the Parkway. The highest elevation on the road through the Smokies is 5,048 feet at Newfound Gap. The campgrounds in Great Smoky Mountains National Park have a reputation for filling up quickly, so arrive early. Gatlinburg is loaded with motels and restaurants.

Smokemont Campground   (828) 497-9270, winter; (828) 497-1000
Smokemont is just 3.8 miles from the southern terminus of the Parkway. Exit right onto US 441.

PART 3:
APPENDICES

Appendix A:
Bicycle Shops

Although we have already listed bicycle shops in our point-by-point descriptions, we thought a directory organized by city would be helpful for anyone needing a quick reference. As you can see, there are very few bike shops spread out over 570 miles. Some of these shops are a considerable distance or change in elevation from the Skyline Drive of Blue Ridge Parkway. Preventive maintenance is in your best interest.

WINCHESTER, VIRGINIA

Blue Ridge Schwinn   (540) 662-1510
From I-81, take the US 50 exit into town. This turns into Jubal Early Road. Turn left onto Loudon Street. Go through two traffic lights and look for shop on left. Open Monday–Friday, 10 a.m.–5 p.m.; Saturday, 10 a.m.–5 p.m.

Element Sports   (540) 662-5744;
www.elementsport.com
From I-81 take exit 313B and go to fourth light. Turn left onto South Pleasant Valley Road and at second traffic light turn into shopping center. Located at 2184 South Pleasant Valley Road, this shop is open Monday–Saturday, 9 a.m.–8 p.m.; Sunday, noon–5 p.m.

WAYNESBORO, VIRGINIA

Rockfish Gap Outfitters   (540) 943-1461;
www.rockfishgapoutfitters.com
1461 East Main Street

Cycle-Recycle Company   (540) 949-8973;
www.cyclerecycle.com
Located 6 miles from the Parkway.

LEXINGTON, VIRGINIA

The Lexington Bike Shop   (540) 463-7969
130 South Main Street

LYNCHBURG, VIRGINIA

Bikes Unlimited Cycling   (434) 385-4157;
www.bikesunlimited.com
2248 Lakeside Drive. This shop is 20 miles from the Parkway east on US 501. Open Monday–Friday, 10 a.m.–7 p.m.; Saturday, 10 a.m.–5 p.m.

ROANOKE, VIRGINIA

Cardinal Bicycle   (540) 344-2453;
www.cardinalbicycle.com
2901 Orange Avenue (US 460 East)

East Coasters, Cycling and Fitness   (540) 774-7933;
www.eastcoasters.com
4341 Starkey Road, near Tanglewood Mall

BOONE, NORTH CAROLINA

Boone Bike and Touring Co.   (828) 262-5750
899 Blowing Rock Road (US 321)

Rock and Roll Sports   (828) 264-0765
280 East King Street

Magic Cycles Inc.   (828) 265-2211;
www.magiccycles.com
140 South Depot Street behind Farmers Hardware

ASHEVILLE, NORTH CAROLINA

Bio-Wheels   (828) 232-0300; www.biowheels.com

Hearns Cycling & Fitness   (828) 253-7851

Liberty Bicycles   (828) 274-2453

Pro Bikes of Asheville   (828) 253-2800;
www.pro-bikes.com

Ski Country Sports   (828) 254-2771
1000 Merrimon Avenue

Carolina Fatz   (828) 665-7744
1240 Brevard Road. Follow NC 191 less than 1 mile
from Parkway.

PISGAH FOREST, NORTH CAROLINA

Back Country Outdoors   (828) 884-4262
Exit 276 South and travel 15 miles to the intersection of
US 64. Look for the lizard on the roof.

Appendix B: For More Information

SHENANDOAH NATIONAL PARK

Superintendent
Shenandoah National Park
Luray, VA 22835-9036
(540) 999-3500
www.nps.gov/shen
Write for maps and information on the Skyline Drive and
Shenandoah National Park.

Shenandoah National Park Association
3655 US 211 East
Luray, VA 22835-9036
(540) 999-3582
www.snpbooks.org
Write for a brochure listing additional books and maps on
Shenandoah National Park.

Shenandoah Valley Travel Association
P.O. Box 1040
New Market, VA 22844
(877) 847-4878
www.svta.org
Write for a directory of facilities in and surrounding Shenandoah
National Park.

BLUE RIDGE PARKWAY

Blue Ridge Parkway Information
199 Hemphill Knob Road
Asheville, NC 28803-8686
(828) 298-0398
www.nps.gov/blri
Write for maps and information on the Blue Ridge Parkway.

Blue Ridge Parkway Association, Inc.
P.O. Box 453
Asheville, NC 28802
(828) 271-4779
Write for a directory of facilities along the Blue Ridge Parkway.

Friends of the Blue Ridge Parkway
P.O. Box 20986
Roanoke, VA 24018
(800) 228-7275
www.blueridgefriends.org
Write for information on how to preserve different aspects of the
Parkway.

Blue Ridge Parkway Foundation
P.O. Box 10427, Salem Station
Winston-Salem, NC 27108-0427
(336) 721-0260
www.brpfoundation.org

STATE TOURISM OFFICES

Virginia Tourism Corporation
901 East Byrd Street
Richmond, VA 23219-4048
(800) 847-4882
www.virginia.org

Division of Travel and Tourism
North Carolina Department of Commerce
301 North Wilmington Street
Raleigh, NC 27699-4324
(800) 847-4862
www.visitnc.com

CHAMBERS OF COMMERCE AND VISITOR/ CONVENTION BUREAUS

North Carolina
Asheville

Asheville Area Chamber of Commerce
151 Haywood Street
Asheville, NC 28801
(828) 258-6101
www.ashevillechamber.org

Asheville Convention & Visitors Bureau
P.O. Box 1010
Asheville, NC 28802
(828) 258-6102; (888) 247-9811
www.exploreasheville.com

Banner Elk

Banner Elk/Avery Chamber of Commerce
4501 Tynecastle Highway
Banner Elk, NC 28604
(828) 898-5605
www.banner-elk.com

Black Mountain

Black Mountain–Swannanoa Chamber of Commerce
201 East State Street
Black Mountain, NC 28711
(828) 669-2300
www.blackmountain.org

Blowing Rock

Blowing Rock Chamber of Commerce
P.O. Box 406
Blowing Rock, NC 28605
(828) 295-7851
www.blowingrock.com

Boone

Boone Area Chamber of Commerce
208 Howard Street
Boone, NC 28607
(828) 264-2225
www.visitboonenc.com

Brevard

Brevard/Transylvania Area Chamber of Commerce
35 West Main Street
Brevard, NC 28712
(800) 648-4523; (828) 883-3700
www.brevardncchamber.org

Burnsville

Yancey County Chamber of Commerce
106 West Main
Burnsville, NC 28714
(800) 948-1632; (828) 682-7413
www.yanceychamber.com

Cherokee

Cherokee County Chamber of Commerce
805 West US 64
Murphy, NC 28906
(828) 837-2242
www.cherokeecountychamber.com

Maggie Valley

Maggie Valley Visitors and Convention Bureau
P.O. Box 87
Maggie Valley, NC 28751
(828) 926-1686
www.maggievalley.com

Sparta

Alleghany County Chamber of Commerce
58 South Main Street
Sparta, NC 28675
(800) 372-5473; (336) 372-5473
www.sparta-nc.com

Spruce Pine

Mitchell County Chamber of Commerce
79 Parkway Road
Spruce Pine, NC 28777
(800) 227-3912, (828) 765-9033
www.mitchell-county.com

West Jefferson

Ashe County Chamber of Commerce
6 North Jefferson Avenue
West Jefferson, NC 28694
(336) 246-9550
www.ashechamber.com

Virginia

Charlottesville
Charlottesville Regional Chamber of Commerce
P.O. Box 1564
Charlottesville, VA 22902
(434) 295-3141
www.cvillechamber.com

Front Royal
Front Royal–Warren County Chamber of Commerce
414 East Main Street
Front Royal, VA 22630
(540) 635-3185
www.frontroyalchamber.com

Galax
Galax–Carroll–Grayson Chamber of Commerce
608 West Stuart Drive
Galax, VA 24333
(276) 236-2184
www.gcchamber.com

Luray
Page County Chamber of Commerce
46 East Main Street
Luray, VA 22835
(888) 743-3915; (540) 743-3915
www.luraypage.com

Roanoke
Roanoke Regional Chamber of Commerce
212 South Jefferson Street
Roanoke, VA 24011
(540) 983-0700
www.roanokechamber.org

The Roanoke Valley Convention and Visitors Bureau
101 Shenandoah Avenue Northeast
Roanoke, VA 24016
(540) 342-6025; (800) 635-5535
www.visitroanokeva.com

Staunton
Greater Augusta County Chamber of Commerce
732 Tinkling Spring Road
Fisherville, VA 22939
(540) 949-8203
www.augustachamber.or

Vinton
Vinton Chamber of Commerce
P.O. Box 83
Vinton, VA 24179
(540) 343-1364
www.vintonva.com

Waynesboro
Waynesboro–East Augusta Chamber of Commerce
301 West Main Street
Waynesboro, VA 22980
(540) 949-8203

Appendix C: Major Elevation Gains

This data, compiled by Tom DeVaughn of Troutville, Virginia, provides you with a quick tally of the gains in elevation along the Blue Ridge Parkway. The chart does two things: It divides the Parkway into sections and adds up the total number of feet climbed within sections. It also specifies at what mileposts major uphills begin and end, with the elevation climbed for each uphill. For example, southbound between Mileposts 4.7 and 8.5, the Parkway has a continuous gain in elevation of 1,100 feet.

Note: Beginning a ride at 3,000 feet and cycling to 4,500 feet does not mean a simple gain of 1,500 feet. The Skyline Drive and the Parkway both rise and fall any number of times before arriving at certain elevations. You may climb the same 500 feet four or five times without any indication on National Park Service maps.

While we provide this chart and the elevation profile graphs in the point-by-point descriptions, we hope you will not be intimidated by elevation. Try not to dwell on the task. Just take in the scenery and enjoy the subtle changes each 500 feet can make.

Mileposts	NORTHBOUND Total Elev. Climbed	NORTHBOUND Major Uphills Mileposts	NORTHBOUND Elevation Change	SOUTHBOUND Total Elev. Climbed	SOUTHBOUND Major Uphills Mileposts	SOUTHBOUND Elevation Change
0–24	1,450 ft.	13.7–10.7	563 ft.	2,810 ft.	0–3	391 ft.
		9.2–8.5	222 ft.		4.7–8.5	1,100 ft.
		4.7–3.0	300 ft.		9.2–10.7	322 ft.
					18.5–23.0	785 ft.
24.0–48.0	2,670 ft.	46.4–43.9	627 ft.	1,742 ft.	37.4–38.8	229 ft.
		40.0–38.8	331 ft.		42.0–43.9	570 ft.
		37.4–34.0	951 ft.		47.0–48.0	177 ft.
48.0–63.0	1,870 ft.	63.0–49.3	1,852 ft.	250 ft.	48.0–49.3	228 ft.
63.0–76.7	0 ft.			3,305 ft.	63.0–76.7	3,305 ft.
76.7–96.0	2,865 ft.	93.1–91.6	374 ft.	1,360 ft.	89.1–91.6	569 ft.
		89.1–87.3	634 ft.		93.1–95.4	428 ft.
		85.6–84.7	230 ft.			
		83.5–76.7	1,490 ft.			
96.0–120.4	2,680 ft.	115.0–113.0	280 ft.	1,657 ft.	118.1–120.4	462 ft.
		106.0–103.6	500 ft.			
		102.5–99.8	820 ft.			

	NORTHBOUND			SOUTHBOUND		
Mileposts	Total Elev. Climbed	Major Uphills Mileposts	Elevation Change	Total Elev. Climbed	Major Uphills Mileposts	Elevation Change
120.4	Mill Mountain Spur—length to summit: 3.1 miles. Elevation climbed from Parkway: 330 ft.			Elevation climbed from Parkway to summit: 580 ft.; elevation climbed from summit to		
120.4–144.0	2,006 ft.	140.1–139.3	229 ft.	3,200 ft.	127.0–132.5	1,400 ft.
		136.0–134.9	285 ft.		134.0–134.9	195 ft.
		124.6–123.1	320 ft.		136.4–138.2	275 ft.
		121.4–120.4	265 ft.			
144.0–168.0	1,840 ft.	159.4–157.6	389 ft.	2,530 ft.	150.6–152.1	278 ft.
		150.6–149.8	226 ft.		157.0–157.6	200 ft.
					164.7–168.0	830 ft.
168.0–192.0	2,445 ft.	189.4–188.7	220 ft.	1,745 ft.	169.5–170.1	260 ft.
		175.1–171.9	575 ft.		176.2–177.0	212 ft.
		168.9–168.0	185 ft.		186.6–188.8	360 ft.
192.0–216.0	2,225 ft.	215.6–214.0	260 ft.	2,047 ft.	195.0–196.2	235 ft.
		210.6–209.4	222 ft.		197.6–198.7	210 ft.
		199.4–198.7	165 ft.		200.5–201.5	335 ft.
216.0–240.0	1,566 ft.	240.0–239.3	160 ft.	2,530 ft.	216.6–217.7	240 ft.

SOUTHBOUND

Total Elev. Climbed	Major Uphills Mileposts	Elevation Change
	231.3–233.1	550 ft.
	233.7–235.2	280 ft.
	235.8–236.9	365 ft.
2,680 ft.	240.0–240.8	170 ft.
	249.0–249.8	235 ft.
	251.3–252.8	300 ft.
	263.6–264.6	360 ft.
3,160 ft.	265.2–266.8	270 ft.
	269.8–271.1	330 ft.
	271.4–273.1	575 ft.
	276.4–277.4	375 ft.
	281.7–282.4	280 ft.
	282.7–283.8	255 ft.
	286.0–287.8	500 ft.
2,210 ft.	288.7–289.9	250 ft.
	291.8–293.8	400 ft.

NORTHBOUND

Mileposts	Total Elev. Climbed	Major Uphills Mileposts	Elevation Change
240.0–264.6	2,625 ft.	238.5–237.2	270 ft.
		220.8–220.1	205 ft.
264.6–288.0	3,050 ft.	257.8–256.8	200 ft.
		248.0–244.5	495 ft.
		243.8–242.9	270 ft.
		242.4–241.5	300 ft.
		285.2–283.8	400 ft.
		279.6–278.8	270 ft.
		276.4–273.1	910 ft.
		269.8–268.6	315 ft.
		268.1–266.8	380 ft.
288.0–312.0	2,185 ft.	309.9–306.5	460 ft.
		305.6–305.0	200 ft.

Mileposts	NORTHBOUND Total Elev. Climbed	Major Uphills Mileposts	Elevation Change	SOUTHBOUND Total Elev. Climbed	Major Uphills Mileposts	Elevation Change
312.0–336.3	3,120 ft.	295.8–293.8	555 ft.	2,705 ft.	298.6–302.1	1,005 ft.
		291.8–289.9	275 ft.		316.4–318.2	380 ft.
		336.3–335.7	215 ft.		318.5–320.7	590 ft.
		327.4–325.8	290 ft.		330.9–332.1	410 ft.
		325.0–320.7	1,210 ft.		332.6–334.5	545 ft.
		316.4–312.4	520 ft.			
336.3–358.5	1,705 ft.	351.9–349.9	565 ft.	4,060 ft.	336.3–338.9	540 ft.
		334.1–341.8	530 ft.		345.4–349.9	1,480 ft.
		339.8–338.9	260 ft.		351.9–355.0	920 ft.
					355.4–358.5	520 ft.
355.4	Spur Road to Mount Mitchell is 4.8 miles in length. Total elevation climbed from Parkway is 1,390 ft.					
358.5–384.0	4,265 ft.	383.5–376.7	1,135 ft.	680 ft.	361.1–364.1	500 ft.
		375.3–364.1	2,535 ft.			
		361.1–358.5	540 ft.			
384.0–408.0	850 ft.	none	3,705 ft.		393.8–396.4	920 ft.
					397.3–399.7	430 ft.

NORTHBOUND

Mileposts	Total Elev. Climbed	Major Uphills Mileposts	Elevation Change
408.0–431.4 (431.4 is the Parkway's highest elev.)	1,835 ft.	426.5–424.8	325 ft.
		423.2–421.6	250 ft.
		415.6–413.2	385 ft.
		411.9–409.6	400 ft.
431.4–469.1	7,470 ft.	469.1–462.2	2,240 ft.
		461.6–458.9	1,000 ft.
		455.7–451.2	1,480 ft.
		443.1–435.5	2,020 ft.
		433.3–431.4	475 ft.
458.2 Spur road		Heintooga from Balsam Mtn.	
		3.6–1.0	860 ft.

Total Uphill Climb North 48,722 ft.

SOUTHBOUND

Total Elev. Climbed	Major Uphills Mileposts	Elevation Change
2,775 ft.	400.3–405.5	965 ft.
	405.7–407.7	745 ft.
	416.8–420.2	1,100 ft.
	423.2–424.8	230 ft.
	426.5–428.2	405 ft.
	429.0–431.4	600 ft.
3,450 ft.	443.1–451.2	2,450 ft.
	455.7–458.9	810 ft.
	Heintooga to Balsam Mtn.	
	0.0–1.0	255 ft.
	3.6–8.6	845 ft.

Total Uphill Climb South 48,601 ft.

Index